A Killing in Antiques

By Bill Knox

A Killing in Antiques

BILL KNOX

PUBLISHED FOR THE CRIME CLUB BY

DOUBLEDAY & COMPANY, INC.

GARDEN CITY, NEW YORK

1981

All of the characters in this book
are fictitious, and any resemblance
to actual persons, living or dead,
is purely coincidental.

Copy 1
1/82
McNaughton
9.95

Library of Congress Cataloging in Publication Data

Knox, Bill, 1928–
  A killing in antiques.

  I. Title.
PR6061.N6K5   1981   823'.914
ISBN 0-385-17625-2   AACR1
Library of Congress Catalog Card Number 80-2967

For Elizabeth

Once again, I must point out that the organisation and methods of the Scottish Crime Squad are different in some minor details from those given in this story.

I know it and the Scottish Crime Squad know it. They want it that way and I thank them for their help.

B. K.

A Killing in Antiques

CHAPTER 1

Annie Campbell was sixty, grey-haired, still a good-looking woman, and would have clouted anyone who called her a servant. She was housekeeper at Drum Lodge, her husband Donald was chauffeur and handyman, and the rest of the staff was a cleaning woman who came in from the village during the day.

Drum Lodge was a modest-sized Scottish country house in the Perthshire foothills. Their employer, known to his few farming neighbours as Fergie Mackenzie, was a widower and the third generation of his family to have lived in the Lodge. The Campbells had worked for him for seven years.

With only one awkward incident. That had been the night Donald Campbell had been stopped by the police while driving his employer's car after a drink too many. A breathalyser test and the rest had been a formality. Donald had lost his licence for a year and Fergie Mackenzie had held his own review of the case . . . then bought Donald a bicycle and told him the garden needed more attention anyway.

But that had been in the summer, eight months back. Now, her kitchen cleared up after the evening meal, her employer staying the night in Edinburgh, Donald gone off on his bicycle to the village for a darts match, Annie Campbell was ready to relax.

Outside it was dark, drizzling, and cold the way evenings often are in the Perthshire hills during March. But it was warm in the kitchen and she'd brought the portable TV set in. One of her favourite programmes, a hospital soap opera, was on that night.

Annie Campbell poured herself a modest glass of her employer's best whisky, took a sip, and went to switch on the TV set.

The front doorbell rang.

"Damn whoever it is," said Annie Campbell with considerable irritation.

Leaving the kitchen, she walked through the house to the front door. Through the glass panelling she saw a figure in police uniform waiting in the shadows of the porch.

Annie Campbell opened the door. Then gasped as the "policeman" stuck a gun hard into her stomach. A face made grotesque by a stocking mask grinned at her.

"Just be a nice sensible lady," said the figure softly.

Annie Campbell, unafraid of either man or devil, was a farmer's daughter. She looked down at the pistol prodding her stomach, saw the safety catch was off, and nodded.

Two more men in stocking masks, wearing dark sweaters and denim slacks, came out of the night. Annie Campbell was hustled back through to her kitchen, shoved into her chair, and tied to it firmly by a length of cord produced by the "policeman."

"You're wasting your time," said Annie Campbell stoutly. "There's no money here. Not unless you want what's in my purse."

One of the trio chuckled. Then gagged her with a length of sticking plaster.

"Not to worry, Ma," said the "policeman."

He scraped her chair round a little so that it was facing the TV screen. He switched the set on and turned up the sound.

Annie Campbell glared at him as he left with the others. The set was on the wrong damned channel.

It was more than two hours later when Donald Campbell pedalled back through the rain from his darts match at the village hotel. He found the front door of Drum Lodge open and his wife still tied to the kitchen chair.

They were a practical couple. Once Annie Campbell had been set free, she drank her glass of whisky at a gulp. Donald Campbell poured himself a quick one to keep her company. Then they tried to telephone the police.

The line had been cut.

"I'll cycle down to the village again," said Donald wryly. He was thinking of the rain, of the two-mile journey there and the other two miles back. "Annie, what the hell were the devils after anyway?"

"Apparently they didn't want *me*. Not that you'd have bothered much," said Annie Campbell grimly. "We'd better look."

The front lounge of Drum Lodge had an unusually bare appearance. A William and Mary side table, a Chippendale bureau, and a set of Sheraton chairs had gone. In the dining room, a full Crown Derby dinner set had been taken from its display cabinet, an array of Georgian silver was missing, and so was a Georgian plate bucket.

Tight-lipped, Annie Campbell led the way to their employer's study. Things there were just as bad. A row of long glass-fronted cabinets had been forced open. Fergie Mackenzie's prized collection of antique firearms, from Brown Bess muskets to old Scottish horse pistols, had vanished.

Annie tried to look on the bright side. She'd miss the bureau and the Sheraton chairs. But the silver had taken a terrible amount of cleaning, the grandfather clocks had been a devil to dust, and what was the use of a dinner set too precious to be used. As for the guns, though she knew they were valuable too, she'd never liked the things.

"I'll be on my way, Annie." Donald Campbell cleared his throat, hesitated, then added, "Eh . . . I won." He saw his wife's blank expression. "I mean at the darts. I'm in the finals now."

Annie Campbell eyed him stonily.

"Bugger your darts," she said.

It was only the second time in her life she'd used the word aloud. The other time—well, even Donald didn't know about that.

Away from Drum Lodge, away from the Perthshire foothills, Fergie Mackenzie was better known as Lord Mackenzie, one of the senior judges of the Scottish High Court. There his nickname was "Bloody Mac"—a terror to counsel, police, and prisoners alike. In his judicial role, it was claimed that the only time he smiled was when he passed sentence.

Fergie Mackenzie wasn't going to be pleased when he heard he'd been robbed. Her eyes strayed to the bare floorboards, and she mentally added a hand-woven cream Chinese carpet to the missing list. No, he wasn't going to be pleased at all.

She glanced at her husband. "Haven't you gone yet?"

"I just thought I'd mention the darts," said Donald, wishing he hadn't. He retreated to the door.

Outside, the rain looked worse than ever.

Most people in the city of Glasgow felt better that Tuesday morning. After almost a week of rain the sun had come back in a clear blue sky. The roads began to dry, spring buds flowered in the city's parks, and even in the worst of her slum tenements life became just that little more tolerable.

Detective Superintendent Colin Thane stood at his office window in the Scottish Crime Squad headquarters building, looked out at the view, and felt reasonably pleased with life. The view, at that moment, consisted mainly of two of the Squad's women officers walking across the parking lot to their unmarked car. Their names were Jill and Jean, both were in their early twenties, slim, good-looking, and wearing loose sweaters and tight, faded jeans.

He grinned. Partly because, although they were both brunettes, they wore blond wigs, partly because he knew they were on their way to top out a month's undercover work by arresting a failed medical student turned disc jockey who had developed a lucrative sideline in blackmail. But mainly because Colin Thane, dark-haired, six feet tall, age forty-two, happily married with two children, maybe not quite as lean as he had once been, still appreciated girls in sweaters and tight jeans.

Jill and Jean got into the car and Thane turned away from the window, going back to his desk. Sitting down, he turned over another sheet of the overnight computer printout lying on his desk.

Two stabbings, an armed holdup, an attempted rape, a solvent-sniffing juvenile found drowned, an old woman left mugged and half-dead . . . the printout only covered Glasgow and was fed through by the city's police. The contents were predictable six days out of seven. Thane shrugged, flicked to the next sheet, then paused as he caught a mention of Millside Division.

Millside Division was an unglamorous, partly dockland chunk of Glasgow. But until three months earlier, when he'd been simultaneously promoted from Chief Inspector to Superintendent and been seconded out of ordinary police work to the Crime Squad, Millside had been Thane's personal patch. The kind of place where being divisional C.I.D. boss meant using your fists at least as often as your brains.

The printout item occupied only four lines, a brief listing of a warehouse burglary. The team had cut a hole in the roof, dropped through, and had carried off about a ton of instant coffee. They'd used a power saw on the roof. Which sounded like Soldier Harris and his sons . . . Thane started to reach for the telephone, then stopped, shaking his head. At least three detectives on the Millside squad were capable of working that out for themselves. An ex-boss shouldn't stick his nose in where it wasn't needed.

He lit one of his tightly rationed supply of cigarettes for the day and glanced at the stainless-steel digital watch on his wrist. They'd given it to him when he left. The engraving on the underside of the casing read: TO THE BOSS, FROM THE MILLSIDE TEAM.

But he was Scottish Crime Squad now, acting second-in-command until Tom Maxwell got back from leave, and a Crime Squad posting was the kind of chance any real cop dreamed about, though few ever realised. A small unit, hand-picked from every force in the country, free from local ties or regional boundaries, financed direct by Central Government, they chose their own targets, which were always major. They used their own methods . . . and more often than not they finished a case before a local cop knew much more than that they might be in his territory.

Still . . . he scribbled the name Soldier Harris on his desk pad, just in case.

The intercom box on his desk chimed softly as he reached for the printout sheet again.

"Come through, will you," said a mild, almost lazy voice, and the intercom went dead again.

Thane stubbed out his cigarette. The summons was from Jack Hart, the Squad commander, and not totally unexpected. Hart, a detective chief superintendent who had been an area C.I.D. chief in Ayrshire before he'd taken over his present job, held a miniature conference session most mornings. That way, he expected to know exactly what was going on. Later, if he found he still didn't, there could be hell to pay.

A quick check down the last two sheets of the printout showed nothing more that mattered. Thane rose and took a brief glance around his room. He still hadn't got used to the carpeting—only superintendents and above rated carpets. The furniture, like the building, was new and modern, which made another change from Millside Division's battered relics. He hadn't done much to the room yet to make it his own, except add a fresh coffee stain to the carpet and accidentally break the coat hook behind the door. But it was beginning to look untidy, more homely.

Going out, he went down a corridor, pressed a button outside the door marked COMMANDER, and an "enter" light flashed. Opening the door, he went in.

"Rest your bones a moment." Commander Hart, a man in his late forties with high cheekbones and a lined, sad-eyed face, nodded from behind his desk. He gestured at the middle-aged, slightly plump and smartly dressed brunette bending over some papers beside him. "Maggie's sorting me out—we're almost finished."

Thane found a chair and settled in it. Maggie Fyffe, the commander's secretary, wore a wedding ring and was a cop's widow. She smiled at Thane, then slid another sheet of paper in front of

Hart. He scribbled his signature, then shoved the collection back towards her.

"Anything else?" he demanded.

"No." Maggie Fyffe glanced at Thane again and seemed amused about something. "Nothing that can't wait."

"Let's leave it that way," said Hart. "No calls for now. Say I'm out. Say I'm—"

"Arranging a funeral?" suggested Maggie Fyffe.

"Yes." Hart chuckled to himself. "That's fair."

She picked up the papers and left, closing the door behind her. Pursing his lips, Hart opened the red cardboard file lying in front of him and frowned at it for a moment.

Thane waited. The commander's office was about twice as big as his own, with a view out across grassland to a heavy fringe of trees. Beyond the trees was a high fence, and the only gate had a guard and a sign which said POLICE TRAINING AREA.

Which it was. The Scottish Crime Squad shared the area with the Strathclyde Mounted Branch, who had their stables in one section, and the Dog Branch, who were inclined to be noisy neighbours. Publicly, the Squad was listed in telephone directories as being in the heart of Glasgow. The polite fiction was maintained by a token presence, but their operational base was here, south of the river, on the fringe of the city, just off the M.8 motorway for Greenock.

Privacy mattered to the Squad. Their mixture of target surveillance and attack strike pattern police work, though it stayed within the rules, was best suited to a low profile most of the time.

"Ready," said Hart suddenly, slapping the folder shut. He eyed Thane in the same odd, almost amused way as Maggie Fyffe had seconds earlier. "What's your opinion of the judges of the High Court of Justiciary?"

"As a breed?" Surprised, Thane shrugged. "They're human, I suppose—some of them, anyway."

Hart chuckled and laid both hands flat on the desk.

"How about the redoubtable Lord Mackenzie, alias Bloody Mac? Ever had that pleasure?"

"Yes." Thane grimaced at the reminder. "I can show you the scars."

It had been a totally unspectacular murder trial, with few complications, but Lord Mackenzie had been in a foul temper from the start. Hunched behind the bench, a sour-faced little figure in judicial wig and scarlet robes, Bloody Mac had reduced both the Advocate Depute for the Crown and defending Counsel to nervous wrecks while he terrorised jury and witnesses alike.

When it was Thane's turn to give evidence, His Lordship leaned forward like a hungry vulture, listened stonily, then criticised every police officer involved before suggesting Thane could be lying.

Later, Bloody Mac's immaculate summing up had flayed the defence story, the jury had brought in a guilty verdict, and the accused had gone down for life. But that particular day was one when Colin Thane would have given a lot to get his hands round a certain scrawny throat.

"I thought so," mused Hart. "There's enough of us to form a club. Still—" He nodded at the folder. "Our friend lives at Drum Lodge, somewhere in the wilds of Perthshire. Two weeks ago the house had visitors on a Saturday night. Unfortunately, Lord Mackenzie wasn't at home—but the housekeeper was tied up at gunpoint, and a team cleaned out thirty thousand pounds' worth of antiques."

"You're interested?" asked Thane with a slight frown.

Hart nodded.

Thane was immediately suspicious. "What's wrong with the local cops?"

"Nothing. But they've drawn a blank." Hart paused, then added with sarcasm, "It happens. Even when there's a High Court judge involved."

"So you're moving in." Thane rubbed a thumb along his chin, his suspicion growing. One of the first rules he'd learned when he joined the Crime Squad was that it steered clear of routine crime, from robbery onward. He eyed Commander Hart innocently. "Someone leaning on us, sir?"

"No, not the way you mean," said Hart frostily, a flush of annoyance on his cheeks. "Even if it was happening, I believe I'm still running this Squad. I—"

He broke off, swinging round in his chair as an excited, high-pitched barking began outside. A moment later a large young Alsatian dog streaked past across the grass, pursued by an irate, uniformed handler. They vanished from sight and the noise died away.

"Dog Branch have some new recruits." Hart swung back, his manner still frosty. "One of the first things they teach the brutes is not to bark too soon. A sensible policy, don't you think?"

Thane nodded.

"Come to that, you'd look at home on the end of a lead—it's a notion." Hart's good humour returned, and he nodded at the folder again. "Colin, there's no direct leaning. The Drum Lodge break-in is simply part of a target package—a package I was asked to work on weeks ago, before Lord Mackenzie lost his goodies." He shrugged. "When a Government minister says he's worried, I pay attention."

That part Thane could easily understand. The Scottish Crime Squad's annual budget would soon be up for review.

"Antique thefts?" It seemed the obvious.

"That's it. An epidemic of them—and a new team, who work like pros and know what they're doing." He shoved the folder across to Thane. "Drum Lodge is just one of eleven jobs in there. Dotted all over the country, but all looking like the same team. They ignore junk, only take the best, and the minimum they've cleared on any one operation is ten thousand pounds, bottom book."

Thane looked at the folder. "Mine?"

"Yes." Hart pursed his lips. "Uh—how much do you know about antiques?"

"Not much," admitted Thane. "Unless you count my car."

It was more accurately his wife Mary's car now. He'd shared

the old station wagon with her, but now, with the Squad transport pool available, she had it most of the time. It had rust, balding tyres, and a thirst for oil.

"That doesn't exactly help," said Hart. "No criticism of you, but it's bad luck Tom Maxwell is on leave."

Thane knew what he meant. Hart's regular deputy, Detective Superintendent Maxwell, walked with a limp because he'd once fallen off a roof while chasing an armed thug. But Maxwell, who had come to the Squad from Edinburgh, liked burrowing in junk shops and sniffing around auction sales. When he got them cheap enough, he collected prints of old sailing ships.

"Couldn't you get him back?" he asked.

"No." Hart's growl made it plain he'd thought of that. "He's touring France, remember? He took his wife, a tent and his car—no contact addresses."

"A pity," said Thane.

He tried not to grin. Tom Maxwell was nobody's fool. He knew that Maxwell had actually left two emergency addresses with Maggie Fyffe, but under blood-curdling threats of what would happen if she told the Squad commander about them.

"So you're stuck with it." Hart put his thin hands together in something roughly resembling an attitude of prayer. Then he brightened. "Hell, antiques or whatever, does it matter? You're still going thief-catching. Except, of course—" He fell silent, contemplating his hands for a moment.

"There's a problem?" asked Thane resignedly.

"Just that we want to dig a little deeper." Hart abandoned prayer. "This outfit needs a market, a crooked buyer. Stolen antiques are always moved fast and far, straight out of the country—that's been known for a long time. The thing is like a pipeline with stolen antiques going in at one end, then coming out at the other end as apparent legitimate deals. I'd bet even money that by now Bloody Mac's stuff is either in Amsterdam or Paris or on its way to some Manhattan showroom."

Thane nodded, wondering why he'd ever thought it was going to be a pleasant day. One of the telephones on Hart's desk buzzed softly. Hart picked up the receiver, listened, then murmured an acknowledgement and hung up.

"Right." Hart made no comment about the call. "You don't look too happy."

"I'm trying to think," said Thane wryly. A memory had stirred, a memory from several years back. "I've one contact in the antiques game—if he's still active."

"I can give you something better." Hart beamed at him. "I heard about it last night and got the summary this morning. It's the reason we're moving in." He thumbed at the folder. "The top sheet."

More barking had begun outside, but further off. A small procession of police dogs and handlers were heading out towards their training ground. They were supervised by a sergeant, who seemed to be making most of the noise. Hart swung round to watch them, scowling, while Thane opened the folder.

The top item was a closely typed report sheet from the Squad's modest-sized "branch office" team based in Edinburgh. Several teleprinter flimsies had been clipped to it. Puzzled, Thane flicked through them—the flimsies came from the Criminal Intelligence unit of Strathclyde Police in Glasgow, from a police division in Edinburgh, and from a traffic police unit in the north of England.

He glanced at Hart. The Squad commander was still making a deliberate business of looking out at the dog parade.

"It's a strange story," said Hart without turning round. "Don't rush it—or the women involved."

"Sir." Thane lit a cigarette, began reading, felt even more bewildered for the first few lines, then gradually became interested.

It had begun about six months earlier. Mrs. Helen Morton, an Edinburgh dentist's wife, had been trying on a new dress in a Princes Street store when her handbag was stolen from the changing cubicle. She lost money, cheque book, credit cards and her driving licence.

A week later a woman named Anna Marshton, single, four

previous convictions, had been caught in a Glasgow department store as she tried to walk off with another customer's handbag.

Anna Marshton lived in Glasgow. Two detectives had gone along to make a routine search of her home, a small apartment in a high-rise low-rent council block where she lived alone. They turned up a small cache of items which tied Anna to handbag snatches in Glasgow and Edinburgh. One item had been Helen Morton's cheque book.

Admitting six charges of theft, Anna Marshton had appeared in court. The duty legal-aid solicitor had made his favorite plea for lost causes, that Anna had been suffering from emotional stress. For once it had worked. Anna had been sentenced to a modest three months' imprisonment.

That meant she'd been out and about for at least two months since. Frowning, trying to keep a timetable in his head, Thane read the next section. It brought the story forward to a Sunday morning. The date had been underlined in ink, with a note added in Jack Hart's neat handwriting: "morning after Drum Lodge break-in."

A truck and a car had collided in a minor traffic accident on the main A.1 coast road south, a few miles over the border into England. A small Volkswagen van coming behind them took avoiding action, skidded off the road, and burst a tyre.

No one was hurt. The crew of a police car, arriving to sort out the accident, discovered the woman driver of the Volkswagen changing the burst tyre. She was a brunette in her early thirties, baldly described by the report sheet as "attractive," and one of the English officers had given her a hand. He noticed the van was carrying a load of old furniture, and the brunette explained she had hired the van and was taking the furniture south to oblige an elderly relative.

The English officer hadn't paid much attention to the load. Thane grinned, with a feeling the cop concerned had probably been more interested in the brunette's legs. But she was a potential witness, and the traffic man had checked her driving licence before she drove off.

The name on the licence was Mrs. Helen Morton, the address in Edinburgh. That went into the traffic crew's accident report, along with the Volkswagen's registration number, where both might have been forgotten. Except that later that day the truck driver in the original accident got back to his depot, complained of feeling ill, then collapsed and died. A postmortem showed he had a hairline skull fracture and had died from a brain haemorrhage.

That meant the accident mattered. A teleprinter request from the English force went to Edinburgh, and two Edinburgh constables were sent around to Mrs. Morton's home to get what seemed a routine statement.

They soon learned differently. Mrs. Morton told them she hadn't stepped outside her home that Sunday. She could prove it. Then, in words a dentist's wife didn't normally use to strangers, she scorched them on their way with a suggestion that police records would show her handbag had been stolen months before and her driving licence had vanished with it.

Two startled constables traced the Volkswagen through its registration number to an Edinburgh van-hire firm. The firm's books showed it had been hired by a women who called herself Helen Morton, who used the driving licence as identification and had paid cash.

The Volkswagen van had been hired on the Saturday and brought back three days later. "Mrs. Morton" had apologised for the burst tyre, had paid cash again to square her account, and they hadn't seen her since. But it wasn't the first time she'd hired one of their vans—always for cash, with the explanation she was secretary of an amateur drama group who sometimes had to move props and scenery.

And the unhappy English traffic cop who helped the fake Mrs. Morton change that wheel could only say that the van had been loaded with old furniture. Which, he supposed, could have been antiques.

There was nothing more. Suddenly Thane realised his cigarette was about to burn his fingers. He stubbed the cigarette on an ashtray, frowned at the report sheet again, and heard Hart chuckle.

"Well?" demanded Hart, leaning on his desk. "What do you think?"

"It fits together," agreed Thane slowly, appreciating the digging that lay behind the report sheet. "Anna Marshton—"

"Is small, fat, forty-six, and looks like the back end of a bus," Hart cut him short, scowling. "She snatches handbags, end." He sucked his teeth in irritation. "The local C.I.D. quizzed her about it on Sunday afternoon—which is our bad luck. She claimed she gave the Morton woman's licence to a stranger in a bar for the price of a drink. All right, the local men reckon she's lying. But they're familiar faces and she doesn't frighten easily. They can't budge her."

"A strange, nasty cop might have better luck," mused Thane.

"Never mind the strange and nasty," countered Hart. "Your usual charm and diplomacy are good enough to frighten most people. Our Anna has to be lying. It's more likely someone paid her to get hold of a driving licence, and spelled out what was needed."

The same notion had just begun to trouble Thane.

"Has she worked Edinburgh before?" he asked.

"Not that we know about," said Hart. "But she stole two handbags on that one trip, both from women about the same age. If I'm right, it was a case of second-time lucky—the other victim doesn't drive."

Thane didn't challenge the Squad commander's reasoning. It matched his own. The van had been hired in Edinburgh, and most hire-drive firms demanded sight of a driving licence as identification. They felt happier with a reasonably local address.

But something else mattered. Every British driver's licence included the holder's date of birth, a piece of sexual equality not every woman liked. The information was hidden in computer coding, but hire-drive staff knew how to read it and usually did, as a routine check.

To be any use, the stolen driving licence had to come from a woman of about the same age as the woman who was going to hire the van. And the stolen licence had been used for more than one hire from the same firm.

"One licence." He glanced at Hart. "If this is our antiques gang, they may have more."

"Try asking Anna Marshton. My guess is they won't use the Morton woman's licence again." Hart shook his head in grudging respect. "If that load of 'old furniture' wasn't from Drum Lodge, it was from some other job, on its way out. Using a hired van makes sound sense—it would be a whole lot safer than something stolen or a set of false plates."

He stopped there and glanced at his wristwatch. Thane took the hint and rose, picking up the folder.

"I'll read this again"—he hefted the folder—"then I'll go and see our bagsnatch lady."

Hart stopped him. "There's someone I want you to talk with first."

"Sir?"

Thane saw the barely disguised grin on the Squad commander's lips and remembered the way Maggie Fyffe had glanced at him. Whatever was coming, Hart had been deliberately saving it.

"Lord Mackenzie thinks he can help." Hart kept a near straight face but was obviously enjoying the moment. "He has some kind of pet theory he wants to talk about."

"With me?" asked Thane weakly.

"With the senior officer handling the case," said Hart. "That's you, and you're in luck. The High Court has a sitting in Glasgow today, and he's presiding in the North Court. I had Maggie check—he'll recess for coffee at eleven and see you then."

"Nice of him," said Thane.

"That's what I thought." Hart's grin broke through. "Uh—he says he remembers you."

Colin Thane didn't return directly to his office. He turned down another corridor, nodding to a detective inspector who emerged from one of the side rooms as he passed.

The man returned the greeting gloomily. His two-year secondment to the Crime Squad had ended. He was going back to his home force in the north, with promotion and a posting to a small county town. The system worked that way. Despite the career benefits, plenty of Squad members reacted sadly when their time came to leave.

The main duty room was at the far end of the corridor, its door open. Going in, Thane glanced around hopefully. It was a large room but, as usual, few of its desks were occupied. Marker pins on the wall maps, which covered all Scotland, showed some of the reasons. But he gave a pleased whistle at the sight of a tall, slim, red-haired girl sitting on her own at the far end of the room.

Seeing him coming, she made a halfhearted display of pushing aside two sugary doughnuts on a paper plate, still holding the remains of another in her right hand.

"I got hungry," she said, brushing away some sugar which had powdered down the denim jacket she wore over a grey shirt and matching trousers. Nodding towards the plate, she suggested, "Try one."

"Another time." Thane grinned. Sandra Craig was a detective constable, was usually found eating, yet never seemed to put on an ounce of weight. "Any idea where Francey or Joe Felix are hiding?"

She nodded. "They went over to the electronics workshop. Joe wanted to show off some new toy they've got." Reaching for the telephone beside her, she asked, "Want them, sir?"

"No." Thane shook his head. "Just you for now."

"Best offer I've had since breakfast," she said cheerfully. "How about Francey and Joe?"

"Tell them not to wander. I'm going to need them."

Thane left it at that, knowing it would be enough. Sergeant Francey Dunbar was young, could be awkward and sometimes mutinous, but had been assigned to Thane. Joe Felix was a middle-aged detective constable in the surveillance and technical section. He and Sandra Craig were the other members of what, more by accident than design, had become Thane's personal team. It was a gradual process, not totally complete, because all had been Crime Squad before Thane arrived—and he knew there were times when they still regarded him as the new boy.

"What have we got?" asked Sandra Craig. "Something good?"

"Maybe." Thane checked the folder he was still carrying. "Starting with a female bagsnatcher. Anna Marshton."

"Her?" The girl raised a quizzical eyebrow. "I know her, from before I came here—back when I was on street duty. What's she supposed to have done?"

"Got into bad company," said Thane. "The address is 680 Harald Street. Ask Glasgow C.R.O. what's on file for her, then meet me out there at noon. I want a talk with her."

Sandra Craig looked puzzled but nodded. As Thane turned to leave, she took another bite from her doughnut, then lifted the telephone.

Lord Mackenzie expected him at eleven, which gave Thane some time in hand. From the duty room, he went back to his office and read his way through the folder's contents. The bulk of the material consisted of summaries of the other antique thefts Commander Hart had mentioned. What was stolen varied—from paintings and porcelain to furniture and silver, even old musical instruments, and sometimes things as heavy as grandfather clocks.

The geographical scatter was something else. Without being certain why, he sensed there was a missing element. Glancing at his watch, he decided that would have to wait, shoved the folder in a drawer, and rose.

On the way out of the building he passed the reception area. Maggie Fyffe was there, behind the outer office counter, a typist working in the background while she sat like a benevolent queen bee with a small bank of external TV scanner screens on one side and a computer terminal keyboard on the other.

"Going out, Superintendent?" she asked innocently.

"Correct," he said dourly. "Maggie, if there were three of you, you'd be a hit in *Macbeth*."

Her laughter followed him out through the glass main door.

The Crime Squad parking lot held a considerable mix of vehicles, an apparent middle-range collection of unmarked makes and models. None had a visible radio aerial, but each carried special low-band transmitter sets with scrambler facilities. Thane's car, a grubby-looking blue Ford Cortina, stayed that way because it was a standing order that vehicles should only go through a car wash once a month. Grubby cars were less likely to be noticed . . . and when the car was finally washed it often had its registration plates changed. That dated back to the Saturday night a young car-spotter, who was also an aspiring juvenile delinquent, had been caught in a Gorbals billiard hall selling typewritten lists of every Crime Squad registration number at five pounds a list.

Getting behind the wheel, Colin Thane set the Ford moving. Driving towards the main gate, he kept his speed down as he met a mounted police detail heading back towards their stables. Hooves clattering, polished harness jingling, the horses were superb animals and mostly imports from Irish bloodstock farms. Their riders sat easy in the saddle, each man wearing white gloves. That meant they'd been on ceremonial duty at the High Court. He smiled as they went past. The only complaint he'd ever heard from a mountie was that they'd a set of cavalry lances in a storeroom but were only allowed to use them at police displays . . . which, faced with the occasional riot at a football match, seemed a waste.

Beyond the line of trees, the main gate opened for him. He waved to the uniformed constable on duty, turned left at the Police Training Area sign, and a minute later was driving on the city-bound side of the M.8, staying with the traffic flow.

He was in no hurry. Bright in the sunlight ahead, the steel and concrete of the Glasgow skyline was something to which he could always instinctively relate, feel at ease with.

A tall, neat, grey-eyed man, wearing a soft Donegal tweed suit, white shirt and plain dark tie, Colin Thane usually had the appearance of being unhurried. He had a rugged, naturally cheerful face and thick dark hair. Years back, when he'd been a

young beat cop in the city, he'd also been a more keen than suc-
cessful amateur boxer—and he still had the muscular build and
ease of movement which trained fighters never totally lose.

What wasn't so obvious, until people worked with him or ex-
perienced it, was that there was another side to Thane's character. There were times when he apparently let instinct take over
under pressure, when he showed an aggressive tendency to back
a hunch and act—an outrageous blend of sometimes stretching
the rules and being prepared to fight dirty if necessary to preserve them.

It was an outlook he'd learned when that young beat cop had
worked a section of Glasgow slumland where getting involved in
at least one back-street brawl was part of every night-duty shift.

But his hunches, his gambles, usually came off. Because they
were more often carefully calculated risks—and one thing he
didn't know was that that had been the factor which had swung
his selection for the Scottish Crime Squad.

At Millside Division he'd been the youngest divisional chief in
the city. As a superintendent he was still ahead of most of his
contemporaries. Typically, he seldom thought about it.

As the mud-spattered blue Ford purred over the Kingston
Bridge, then left the motorway on the north side of the Clyde,
Thane's thoughts were on something totally different. Lord
Mackenzie would probably be not much more than a public-
relations exercise. But if Anna Marshton wouldn't talk, where
the hell did he go from there?

Glasgow's High Court of Justiciary building is a squat Greek-
Doric bulk of grey stone beside the River Clyde. It sits opposite
Glasgow Green, a stretch of bedraggled parkland which the sensible citizen avoids after dark, leaving it to the city's sad human
debris who have nowhere else to go and the occasional small
packs of vicious young predators seeking easy prey.

There was parking space beside the river. Thane squeezed the
Ford into a gap and got out. A man in working clothes was
standing a few feet away, watching with an apparently casual

disinterest, disinterest which didn't quite match the slight bulge of a gun under his donkey jacket or the two backup men waiting further along the street.

The man, a detective from Central Division, recognised him and grinned.

"Slumming, sir?" he asked.

"Earning my corn." Thane glanced at the backup men. "Problems?"

"A bomb threat." The man shrugged. "We don't think it's for real." He yawned slightly. "At least it isn't raining."

Thane nodded and crossed towards the Justiciary building. He hadn't bothered to remark on the gun. Though the average Scottish policeman still carried nothing more lethal than a short wooden baton and a notebook, firearms issue was no longer something which raised ire or eyebrows.

Particularly around the Justiciary building. Recently it had just survived a fire-bomb attack. Two known plans for armed attempts to free prisoners had been thwarted. There had been other bomb threats, a series of trials involving political terrorists of a variety of shades, a general climate in which security needs had escalated far above having a few uniformed men standing around.

The High Court hadn't faltered in its function—or its traditions. It still had two splendidly garbed State Trumpeters to open each sitting with a fanfare, a minister of religion to ask a solemn blessing on its proceedings, a small-stakes poker game going in the basement pressroom. If there was a new tradition under way of having an armed marksman on the roof, Thane hoped someone would remember to feed him now and again.

A girl wearing a sheepskin jacket was collecting for charity at the foot of the main courthouse steps. She was young and good-looking, probably the reason why she hadn't been moved on by the two blue-uniformed constables standing at the door, and as he fed some change into her collecting can she smiled and pinned a small flag to his lapel.

Thane climbed the steps, passed the constables, and went in

through the doors in the Greek-Doric entrance portico. The outer hall, an area of black-and-white marble, held a thin scattering of wigged and gowned advocates, gossiping lawyers and one or two pressmen. He recognised most of them. The High Court was a club where you paid your membership dues in sheer waiting time, and from the signs he guessed the North Court had just gone into recess.

"Mr. Thane." The black-gowned man who came towards him was a clerk of court, and looked relieved. "Lord Mackenzie told me to meet you. He's waiting."

Thane followed as the clerk, gown swishing, led the way along a broad central corridor. The walls on either side were lined with a long panelled frieze preserved from an even earlier building. It told the story of justice in Athenian style, from a chained prisoner being brought in, through his trial, to a judge pronouncing sentence and an executioner standing ready with an axe. Eyeing them as he walked, Thane had a feeling Bloody Mac probably regretted he couldn't have a man with an axe in the wings.

At the end of the corridor they reached the judges' private area, and the clerk stopped at a polished mahogany door.

"How's his mood?" murmured Thane as the clerk knocked on the door.

"If he was in a cage, you'd feed him raw meat," said the clerk softly. He winced as a muffled growl answered his knock. "For God's sake don't ruffle him. I've got him for the rest of the day."

He opened the door, waved Thane through, but didn't follow. As the door closed again, Thane met the gaze of a small man in his late sixties who sat like a hunched gnome in the depths of a large leather armchair.

"Yes, I thought I remembered you," said Lord Mackenzie with satisfaction, rising. "The case of a man Garrison. You gave interesting evidence—a chief inspector then, weren't you?"

"Sir." Thane nodded. He met the judge's penetrating blue-eyed gaze. "I remember it too."

"Do you?" The man they called Bloody Mac gave a wintery

smile. He had close-clipped grey hair, a thin, leathery face, and dentures which gave an occasional disconcerting click. He wore a plain dark suit with a starched white wing collar and white cravat. His ermine-trimmed robes of office and judicial wig were abandoned on a desk, and he wasn't alone.

A fair-haired man in his early thirties stood at a table nearby, slipping papers into a briefcase. He looked up at Thane and smiled.

"I'm just leaving," he said cheerfully. Then his green eyes noticed the charity flag in Thane's lapel and he glanced at Lord Mackenzie. "Another willing supporter?"

"You know about the Ransom Trust, Superintendent?" asked Mackenzie.

"I've heard of it." Thane glanced at the charity flag. It showed an empty wheelchair, nothing more.

"Your average citizen. Rattle a collecting can and he'll give, no questions," said the stranger sadly. He was about medium height with a slim build and an almost boyish face. "It's what I keep saying. We need to be better known."

"Quite." Lord Mackenzie gestured indulgently. "Superintendent, this is Peter Barry. I—ah—am the Trust's Scottish chairman. Peter's sister is secretary."

"And I'm honorary errand boy," said Barry with mock disgust.

"Ransom—" Thane had a wisping recollection. "You're into medical research."

"We sponsor research into children's diseases," explained Barry. "That doesn't come cheaply, isn't dramatic enough to get much publicity. Right now we're on a fund-raising campaign—collections, fund-raising events right across Scotland." He snapped the briefcase shut and nodded to Mackenzie. "That's it, then, sir. Shona will have this lot ready for tomorrow. Anything else?"

Lord Mackenzie shook his head. "That's everything. Are you going back to Edinburgh now?"

"I've a couple of business calls first." Barry grimaced wryly at Thane. "In between times, I try to earn a living—it isn't easy."

Nodding goodbye, he lifted the briefcase and went out. As the door closed behind him, Lord Mackenzie said, "That was unexpected but necessary. Peter can be—ah—somewhat unpredictable in his appearances." His dentures punctuated the sentence with a click. "Still, I could almost have asked him to stay. He has a reasonable knowledge of our common interest, Superintendent."

"The antiques world?"

Lord Mackenzie nodded. "His late father was an authority, his sister is an expert on silver—Peter's interests are more in the commercial world." He left it at that, nodding towards a coffeepot and cups on the desk beside his robes. "Help yourself. I don't indulge. Not when I think of my age, my bladder, and two hours on the bench before lunch recess."

Thane chuckled. Lord Mackenzie gave enough of a frown to show he saw no reason for amusement, watched Thane pour a cup of coffee, then gestured towards a chair opposite his own. As they sat down, Thane took a quick glance around the room.

It was large, suitably masculine—unlike lesser courts, the Senators of the College of Justice had not yet seen fit to invite a woman into their ranks—and tastefully furnished from the leather upholstered chairs to paintings on the walls, thick carpets, and a small dining table. But slightly shabby.

There were plans for a new court building. It was overdue. The jury room was a cramped slum, the witness rooms worse, the prisoners' cells in the basement one stage better than dungeons. But in a time of financial cutbacks, the money needed wasn't going to be found easily.

"You know why you're here." Lord Mackenzie produced a thin cheroot from a waistcoat pocket and lit it with a slim gold lighter. "My role—" he drew on the cheroot, then used it as a pointer—"my role in the affair is purely that of an ordinary private citizen. I want that understood."

Thane sipped the coffee, saying nothing.

"Do you know anything about antiques?"

"No," admitted Thane. He wondered how many times that question was going to be asked before he was finished.

"It makes you no worse than many who think they do," said the little man acidly. "One piece of advice in that area, Superintendent. The antiques world has its quota of—ah—fragile personalities. To some of them a raised voice would constitute police brutality. At the same time I could name several who are as hard as granite when they see something they want—including a few women."

"I'll remember." Thane eyed him mildly. "And your category?"

"An interested amateur." Lord Mackenzie drew on the cheroot again. "I've dabbled, that's all—and what I've lost I don't expect to see again, barring a miracle."

"You had insurance cover?"

Lord Mackenzie nodded. "Not totally up to current values. But fairly adequate in money terms." He shrugged. "I spent fifteen years collecting antique firearms, as and when I could afford them—that's what I can't replace."

"We might get lucky," said Thane.

"Save that for soothing your average outraged citizen," snapped Mackenzie impatiently. "We both know better. You realise, I presume, that these villains appear to be staying deliberately low-key?"

"Low-key?" Thane straightened in surprise. "They took you for thirty thousand pounds' worth!"

"Don't interrupt." For a moment, the full courtroom Bloody Mac showed through. "Every theft in their operation has involved some small, insignificant collection, my own included. Damn it, man—I could take you to any number of private collections worth ten times as much and still considered unexceptional. Or to funny little back-street museums where the trustees worry about paying the caretaker's wages but could sell out for a king's ransom. That's one of the things I wanted to tell you."

"Interesting." Thane meant it. "That way, and with robberies scattered over the country—yes, they don't attract too much attention." Or wouldn't have, but for the sniffing and collating that went on in the Crime Squad building.

"There's an alternative," said Lord Mackenzie grimly. "Perhaps they've simply been rehearsing for bigger things to come."

"Perhaps." It seemed a safe, neutral word.

"One of them is an expert in antiques." Lord Mackenzie hesitated, seemed to burrow deeper into his armchair, and for a moment his gaze seemed fixed on a watercolour landscape on the opposite wall. "By that, I mean they have more than just good information at their disposal. I have a painting on the wall of my study at Drum Lodge. I call it my Degas—does the name mean anything to you?"

"I've been in art galleries," said Thane unemotionally. "Being a cop, it was usually to get in out of the rain."

"I deserved that." The man opposite almost smiled. "Well, people visit, people admire my Degas—a few who should know better have even wanted to buy it. Yet the truth is that my Degas is a forgery, a skilled fake—and I expect you to respect that confidence. Very few people know. My reasons for keeping my forged Degas, preserving its secret, are—well, personal, sentimental if you wish."

"I don't put everything on a report sheet," said Thane.

"I seem to recall that. So—why was it left behind by my visitors when everything else of apparent value in that room was carried off?"

Taken off guard, Thane shook his head. There had been paintings taken in some of the raids. He knew that from the Crime Squad folder.

"The people who do know—" he ventured cautiously.

"For sure?" A sardonic edge came into Lord Mackenzie's voice. "Only three. I think I can vouch for them." He ticked his fingertips as he went on. "There's my late wife's sister—she lives in New Zealand. There's the solicitor who holds my will, a lifelong friend. And the man who painted it, who now happens to be a highly respected artist in his own right."

"No one else?" Thane frowned. "Some visitor—"

"It's a good forgery," said Lord Mackenzie.

A bell began ringing somewhere outside, a signal that the

North Court's recess time was over. The jury would be filing back in, advocates and pressmen having a quick last draw on their cigarettes, the prisoner being brought back up to the dock. There was a gentle knock at the door, it opened a little, and the clerk of court stuck his head round the edge. Before he could speak, Lord Mackenzie scowled and waved a hand in dismissal. The door closed again.

"Justice calls," said Lord Mackenzie. He rose from his chair. "I'm free tomorrow—a trial postponed due to a vanishing witness. I'd like to talk to you again, Thane, and you might find it useful. Could you drive through to Drum Lodge, about midmorning?"

"Yes." Thane got up, watching as the spare figure slipped into his judicial robes. "I need any help I can get."

"Good." Mackenzie gave a satisfied nod. "I'm also squeezing in a Ransom Trust committee meeting at noon—hence the confusion when you arrived. But we should have time enough before that." Picking up the long, old-fashioned judicial wig, he crammed it on his close-clipped grey head. The transformation was awesome, and Bloody Mac's lack of inches was suddenly without significance. "One last thing before you go, Superintendent—"

"Sir?" Thane felt as if the temperature had taken a sudden drop, there was such a change in the man's voice.

"That man Garrison—the last time you gave evidence in my court," said Lord Mackenzie softly. "He was guilty, of course. But I queried your evidence."

"I remember," said Thane.

"One thing puzzled me. On the night he was arrested, the police had stopped his car because of a faulty taillight or some such nonsense." Bloody Mac's dentures clicked derisively. "But for that—ah—fortuitous incident, he might have gone free. Strange, that failed lamp. Wouldn't you agree?"

"It happens, m'lud," said Thane gravely.

He'd slipped into the courtroom style of address without thinking. For the rest—he wasn't likely to forget Garrison. Garrison had embezzled a fortune and had killed a man in the process. He had been about to cut and run, and the police had needed a few more hours before there would be enough evidence to hold him.

The rain had been hosing down that night when Thane had crawled across a carpark to unscrew that tail-lamp bulb. Afterwards, when Garrison had been stopped—he fought down a grin.

"Fate, I suppose." Bloody Mac's voice was frosty. "But I'd rather it happened in someone else's court next time. Of course, you don't know what I'm talking about, do you?"

"No, m'lud," said Thane politely.

Crossing over, he opened the mahogany door.

"You're a reasonably convincing liar, Superintendent," said Bloody Mac softly. "Using our American cousins' deplorable slang, it'll be entertaining to see how you make out as a bull in a china shop—I just hope nothing too expensive gets broken."

CHAPTER 2

The girl flag-seller was gone when Colin Thane left the High Court building. A light wind had begun rippling the bravely planted beds of spring flowers at the entrance to Glasgow Green, and he gave a suspicious glance at a few unwelcome flecks of grey cloud starting to appear overhead.

It was still pleasantly warm. Further down the road some young children were playing a noisy pavement game outside the city mortuary. The driver of a heavy tanker lorry, part of the traffic rumbling past, had stripped to his vest. A young couple held hands as they emerged from a walk across the Green. Only a cluster of old women, gathered as usual near the main entrance in case anything interesting happened, seemed unaffected. Summer or winter they wore their heavy coats and headscarves and clutched the large empty shopping bags which lent a respectability to their vigil.

Thane got back to his car. Starting it up, he switched on the low-band radio and caught the end of a transmission, a woman's voice. The twins had collected their blackmailer and were delivering him to the divisional police station.

That was routine. The Crime Squad didn't have cells of its own. Prisoners were deposited at the nearest local police station. A local force was always invited to mop up its own patch and take care of the paperwork, its Crime Squad visitors more than willing to ease out of any limelight.

The radio murmured other messages as Thane drove through the city, heading east towards the Harald Street area. He handled the car mostly by reflex, his mind partly on the best way to tackle Anna Marshton about her bagsnatching activities but often going back over his interview with Lord Mackenzie.

That had been more useful than he'd expected. Easier too—he grinned, thinking of the judge's embarrassed mention of his forged Degas.

If Mackenzie felt another meeting would be useful, that was that. Thane didn't object. He'd been fascinated at the brief glimpse he'd had of the hitherto hidden side of the dreaded judge's personality.

Not that it had been too much of a surprise. Thane had known other apparent scourges of humanity who behaved very differently off duty.

People like Peter Barry, who only dealt with the other Lord Mackenzie, probably wouldn't have recognised him on the bench. Barry might be just another amiable part-time do-gooder, but Mackenzie had said he also knew about antiques.

A hell of a lot of people did. Lord Mackenzie's forged Degas, left behind, certainly proved that that included the antiques gang—

He broke off with a curse as a woman suddenly pushed a pram onto the road ahead. Braking hard, almost feeling a bus behind him skid to a shuddering halt practically up the Ford's exhaust, Thane scowled as he saw the woman blithely gain the opposite pavement and use the pram to carve a way through other shopping pedestrians.

Maybe he didn't know much about antiques, but it looked like he was going to learn. The thought stayed with him as he drove on, skirting the fringe of the city's business section and going round past the domed bulk of Glasgow Cathedral.

Mary had a pair of old brass farmhouse candlesticks at home, family heirlooms which had belonged to her grandmother. They were his wife's pride, they were probably worth money. He'd wondered how much a few times.

Scratch the average citizen, and he'd probably bet money that a Glasgow cop regarded culture as keeping up with the sports news. The average citizen preferred to believe it that way.

Glasgow was the kind of city that felt happier talking about football than about the magnificence of its art galleries and the reputation of its universities. That wasn't sure if it should really admit to possession of one of the best opera houses in Europe. It took a perverse pride in being regarded by outsiders as a hard, grimy industrial centre—which it was, though one which also possessed some of the finest surviving Victorian architecture in Britain.

Forty miles away to the east and the nation's capital, the rival city of Edinburgh went to the other extreme. It loved its rich history and traditions, its International Festival, the tourist attractions which began with an ancient castle and a Royal palace. It preferred to say much less about its factory chimneys and industrial estates, twitched uneasily at the suggestion it had a crime rate.

The result was a generations-old feud, never too serious, but kept well fuelled by a studied exchange of insults.

Including a sardonic libel, which made him grin as it wisped through his mind—that Glasgow threw out her rubbish but Edinburgh just kept opening antique shops.

The start of a sprawl of high-density housing appeared ahead, his destination. In another moment he was driving through an area where the buildings, though not old, looked grubby and down-at-heel. The sun, angling down, glinted on a faint frosting on the roadway which was broken glass powdered by traffic—and each corner had its group of loafing, out-of-work teenagers who eyed the world with a total disinterest. Even the shop fronts looked neglected and dull.

Harald Street was in the middle of that. Thane steered the Ford into it, slowed to a crawl as he cruised between parked vans and rusted cars, then gave up checking street numbers as he saw a small red Mini stopped at the kerb halfway down.

Pulling in, he got out and locked his door under the disappointed gaze of two school-age boys in sweatshirts and faded jeans. As they shrugged and wandered off, one deliberately swinging a set of jump wires in his hand, Thane walked over to the Mini.

The passenger door swung open and he got in, raising a slightly surprised eyebrow at the driver.

"Who suggested you come along?" he asked suspiciously.

"I'm hiding, sir." Sergeant Francey Dunbar shifted the wad of gum he was chewing from one cheek to the other and grinned at him from behind the steering wheel. Dunbar was slim, just over medium height, and in his twenties. He had a mop of jet-black hair, a strong nose, and a wide, humorous mouth framed by a thin straggle of moustache. "Joe Felix was trying to give me a one-man lecture on the microchip—even work's better than that."

Thane grunted. Once Felix captured an audience and started explaining technology, everything came to a halt.

"Where's Sandra?" he asked.

"In there." Francey Dunbar nodded ahead, to a small shop further down the street. "Chatting up the local gossip factory."

"She told you why we're here?"

"You could put it that way." Dunbar rubbed his long fingers round the steering wheel. In the process, the heavy silver identity bracelet on one wrist gave a metallic jingle. The name tab on it was blank. "She said you didn't exactly spell it out in detail."

"That's right."

Thane wasn't deceived by the innocence in Dunbar's expression. His sergeant, who wore an old suede safari jacket over a black rolled-neck shirt, tan whipcord slacks and wrinkled leather boots, didn't make life particularly easy for himself or anyone around him. Meaning he could be obstinate, supported causes usually lost before they started, and was liable to spend the occasional overnight at a meditation camp if the right girl would be there too. But Francey Dunbar could also stay loyal until it hurt, and Thane had his own way of coping with the rest.

"So?" Dunbar gave up nursing the steering wheel. "When do we hear?"

"It can wait." Sandra Craig had emerged from the little shop, munching a chocolate bar. She vanished from sight for a moment as a heavy garbage truck swung in from the street and passed in front of her, going down a service lane leading to the rear of the building. As the girl appeared again, coming towards them, Thane reached for the car door. "Stay and keep an eye open. Some of the juveniles around here would steal the wheels from under you. And Francey—"

"Sir?" Dunbar raised an eyebrow.

"The story is in my desk when you get back. Read it, then brief Sandra and Joe Felix."

"Right." Dunbar was pleased.

Sliding out of the car, Thane met Sandra Craig as she slipped what was left of the chocolate bar into her shoulder bag.

"Over there, sir—fourth floor." She nodded at the tenement block immediately across the street. "Anna Marshton should be home all right. The old witch who runs that shop says she doesn't usually surface until afternoon."

"We'll find out." Thane led the way across the street. "Anything more?"

"Not much. My old witch says she prefers male cops." Sandra Craig gave an amused grimace. "Maybe Francey should have tried his luck. But she saw Anna Marshton early on Sunday afternoon, when she bought cigarettes." She glanced at Thane. "Anna made some vague noises about maybe taking a holiday, going away for a spell."

"Getting out?" Thane wasn't surprised at the possibility.

They reached the entrance to the tenement block and went in, their feet sounding noisily on the hard concrete underfoot. Glasgow called tenement entrances "closes," and in old tenements a close had tiled or painted walls. But Harald Street had been built in the concrete age, and the grey walls were a mass of spray-painted, mostly obscene graffiti, aimed at everything from religion and police to purely personal insults.

"Limited vocabulary." Sandra eyed the slogans with some disappointment. She thumbed at one, which suggested where someone called Big Andy should shove his head. "Difficult."

"Downright acrobatic," said Thane solemnly.

They headed for the stairway, the stale smell of the building in their nostrils. A thin, middle-aged woman was coming down, an empty shopping bag in one hand. She passed them quickly, sparing them a quick sideways glance, but her expression making it plain that if they didn't want to know about her then she didn't want to know about them.

Four flights up. Sandra Craig tackled them with her long-legged stride and Thane kept up with her gloomily. It was an old, sad, strangely true police legend that there had never in history been a villain who lived on the ground floor.

Each landing had four house doors and a central rubbish-chute hatch. The window on the first landing had been bricked up, the graffiti died out on the second landing as if spray-tin artists found the air too thin at that height. They passed a couple of emptied solvent glue tins. Teenage sniffers sometimes preferred to use a landing. It offered more shelter than a backyard.

One of the house doors on the fourth floor was opening as they reached the landing. It slammed shut again at the sound of their footsteps. Thane grimaced at Sandra, then checked the name-plates. Anna Marshton's was the third door along. He pressed the bellpush beside it, heard a buzzer rasp on the other side, waited, then tried again. There was still no movement.

"Maybe she's out," said Sandra.

"Too early, unless she's working." The voice, a woman's, came from behind them. They turned. The door which had slammed earlier had opened a few inches. The woman looking at them through the gap was in her thirties, with dyed blond hair and a tired face. "Police?"

Thane nodded.

The door eased shut, a guard chain rattled free, and then the woman stepped out onto the landing. She wore old jeans and a grubby sweater and spared Sandra a brief glance before she switched her attention to Thane. Her forced smile would have been more effective if her teeth had been better.

"What's Anna been up to this time?" she asked. "You're the second lot of cops here in two days."

"We want to talk to her, that's all," said Thane. He pushed the bellpush again as he spoke.

"I'm Betty Fisher—" The woman paused invitingly, gave a slight shrug at Thane's lack of response and tried Sandra instead. "I suppose Anna could have been overnighting somewhere. She usually tells me, but—"

"She's a friend?" asked Thane.

The woman considered. "No. But we're both on our own—my man went to a football match two years ago and didn't come back." She frowned at Anna Marshton's door. "You're not lifting her?"

"Not this time," said Thane.

"But she's in some kind of trouble?" The woman hesitated. "I keep my nose out of her business. But she knows some real hard men—gets visitors now and then."

"You mean she's on the game?" asked Sandra Craig bluntly.

"Only when the rent's overdue—you know how it is." The bad teeth showed briefly, then the blonde frowned at the door again. "Maybe I should make sure, in case anything is wrong. I've got a key."

She went inside her door again and returned holding a key. Putting it in Anna Marshton's lock, she glanced at Thane.

"This is for her, not you. Understand?"

Thane nodded.

The key turned, the door swung open, and the woman peeped round it cautiously.

"We'll do it," said Thane firmly, pushing past her, Sandra at his heels.

"Hey—" The woman's voice hit a strident note of protest. "You can't—"

They ignored her.

Anna Marshton's home was a shabby, untidy place which looked as though it hadn't seen paint or wallpaper since the day it was built. A bedroom, a living room, a tiny kitchen, and an even smaller bathroom led off the small hallway. The curtains were closed in the living room, where the window looked down

on the backyard of the building. Thane jerked them open and
the daylight flooded into the sparsely furnished room.

A threadbare couch faced a large TV set which was topped by
a glass vase holding some faded artificial flowers. An almost
empty bottle of whisky and an unopened bottle of gin sat on a
battered sideboard, next to a framed wedding photograph. Picking up the photograph, Thane glanced questioningly at the
blond woman, who had followed them in.

"That's her," she said. "They split up years ago—no kids.
Luckier than me. I've got three."

Sandra Craig returned from a tour of the other rooms and
shook her head.

"Her bed wasn't slept in," she reported. "There are dirty
dishes for one in the kitchen, sir. And a couple of used drinks
glasses."

"Right." Thane picked up a newspaper lying on the couch. It
was two days old and folded open at the TV programmes. He
sighed, heard the rumble of an engine in the backyard, and went
over to the window. Down below, the garbage truck he'd seen
earlier was now at the rear of the building. As he watched, the
truck's hydraulic arms locked onto the metal skip at the bottom
of one of the garbage chutes, lifted it, emptied it into the truck,
then lowered it back in place again. As the truck's crew disen-
gaged the arms and prepared to move on, he turned round.

"When was the last time you saw her?" he asked the blonde.

"Not yesterday." The woman moistened her lips uneasily. "I
took the kids over to see my sister, didn't get back till late. It was
the day before, mister. Sunday." She darted an almost frightened
glance at Sandra. "You said two glasses. We had a drink together—"

"What time?"

"The evening, about eight." She bit her lip. "I didn't stay long.
Anna was in a great mood, but I got the notion she was expecting someone. So—well, you take a hint, right?"

"It's neighbourly," agreed Thane dryly. "What did Anna talk
about?"

"The co—the police who'd been up that morning." The blonde brushed back a stray lock of brittle hair with one hand. Her fingernails were filthy. "She didn't much make sense to me, though. She said it was the first time any of their kind had done her a good turn."

"Meaning?"

The woman shrugged. "I asked her, mister. She just poured me another drink. But I reckoned there was money in it somewhere. Last thing she said, as I was goin' out the door, was that she might try moving down to London for a spell." Those teeth showed again as she grimaced. "London? I told her there was no way I'd want that. The place is too full of foreigners for my liking and—"

Thane stopped her. "She didn't say anything else?"

"No." The blonde looked round the room again. "You think she's—"

"I think you can go back to your own place," said Thane. "We'll look in before we leave."

She left reluctantly. Sandra Craig saw her to the door, closed it firmly, then came back into the living room. Seeing the pensive expression on Thane's face, she waited silently. Outside, the engine of the garbage truck rumbled again as it emptied another of the rubbish containers.

"There's a smell about it," said Thane. Going over to the sideboard, he eyed the wedding photograph moodily. It showed Anna Marshton as a plump, dark-haired bride. The man beside her was thin, smartly dressed and had a slightly nervous grin. It was a happy photograph, but wedding pictures usually looked that way. It was what happened afterwards that mattered. "All right, we turn the place over."

Sandra Craig nodded. "What are we looking for?"

"Anna Marshton knows a name, one we need. Two local cops talk to her, and maybe foul things up." That was unfair, and he knew it, but he was more thinking aloud than explaining. "If they gave her the notion of how to make some easy money, if the notion maybe blew up in her face—" He was reluctant to go on from there, but a gut feeling he didn't like was growing by the minute. "We're looking for money, a name on a piece of paper, a phone number—hell, anything that might help."

They stayed together, checking the bedroom first. As he worked, Thane noted the quiet, thorough way the red-haired girl went about her share of the task. Francey Dunbar, waiting in the car outside, probably wouldn't have thought to check into the toes of a pair of shoes lying under the dressing table. Sandra Craig found twenty pounds in cash jammed into each of them.

When you lived in a place like Harald Street, you took precautions.

They kept on. A brown coat with a cheap fur-trimmed collar was hanging on a peg behind the door. A patch of white on the lapel caught Thane's eye. It was a Ransom Trust collection flag, like the one still in his own lapel.

He checked the coat pockets and dredged out some used paper tissues, an empty, crumpled cigarette packet and a grubby handkerchief. Turning away, he moved past the bed and his foot brushed against something which was soft and yielding.

Stooping, he lifted an imitation-leather handbag. The metal clasp fastening lay open, the contents ready to spill out. Laying the bag on the bed, Thane rummaged through lipstick and a plastic powder compact, more used tissues, a purse with a few pounds and loose change, and a tube of aspirin.

"Sandra." He waited until Sandra Craig came over. "Think she'd forget to take her handbag?"

"Your average woman wouldn't." She sat on the bed for a moment, frowning. "But your average woman has more than one, sir. What about—well, a doorkey?"

He tried again, but there was no key.

Leaving the girl to finish the bedroom, Thane went through to start in the living room. He could hear the garbage truck still rumbling at work outside, and the muffled sound of music from a radio was coming from somewhere nearer, in the tenement.

There was an old glass bowl on the sideboard, beside the wedding photograph. It held oddments from pieces of rolled-up string onward—and a key. He knew it was maybe late to start worrying about fingerprints, but he used his handkerchief to lift the key, took it through to the front door, tried it in the lock, and it fitted.

Closing the door again, he put the key back in the bowl and started on the sideboard drawers. Sandra came through from the bedroom and he told her to start in the kitchen.

He finished with the sideboard, checked around the rest of the room, and could hear the girl occasionally rattling crockery or moving tins. They finished about the same time.

"Nothing." Sandra came back and flopped down on the couch, disgust on her face. "Except there's a resident rat in there—I could hear it moving." She looked up at Thane. "What now? Do we wait?"

He'd been asking himself that. Already, as things stood, he'd gone further than the average court would have appreciated.

"I could talk to her neighbour again," volunteered Sandra Craig, puzzled at his silence.

He was going to agree. But the doorbell sounded. As they glanced at each other it sounded again and kept on, an unbroken, urgent buzz.

Thane got to the door, opened it, and Francey Dunbar almost fell into the little hallway. He was breathing hard, as if he'd run all the way up from street level, and his thin, tanned face had a sickly pallor.

"That garbage truck—" He gasped for breath, staring at Thane. "They've found a body. It's messy. Really messy."

Sergeant Francey Dunbar was never happy when it came to blood. But he looked as near to throwing up as he sounded. Sprinting through to the living room, Thane looked down from its window into the backyard.

Another rubbish container was tilted high on the garbage truck's hydraulic arms, half-emptied into the waiting maw. But the truck engine had stopped. Two of the crew were beside the container, staring into it as if hypnotised.

The spilling trash had parted to expose the body of a woman.

A body visible from the waist upward, still surrounded by vegetable peelings, old newspapers, and all the other discarded detritus of tenement life. But it was easy to understand why Sergeant Francey Dunbar felt sick. The rest of the dead woman's body was caught deep in the steel jaws of the truck's crusher unit, where rubbish was compressed and packed back for maximum payload.

An inquisitive housewife emerged from the tenement. She walked over to the truck and reached it before the crew noticed her.

She screamed. Even four floors up, the sound cut like a knife.

"God Almighty," said Thane, and turned away from the window.

It was Anna Marshton. She had died wearing a green cotton dress and a knitted wool cardigan. Her eyes bulged, her mouth was grotesquely twisted by a displaced dental plate, and her dark hair was matted with greasy food scraps from a burst waste bag.

The postmortem to establish cause of death was likely to be a formality. A length of thin blue nylon cord had been tied tightly around her neck, so tightly that it was almost buried in the swollen flesh.

Standing beside the truck, the stink of its contents invading his nostrils, Colin Thane listened more impassively than he felt while the driver told his story.

The container the crew had been emptying served the rubbish chute for Anna Marshton's tenement close. One loader always stood ready when a container was being tipped, keeping an eye on what was going through the crusher.

He had seen Anna Marshton's corpse slide into view. Now he had gone off to find a drink, the stiffest drink he could get.

"Shook him up, like," said the driver, a wizened little man in overalls who had to be in his sixties. He scratched the three-day stubble of beard on his chin. "Pal, I've done twenty years on midden wagons an' never had this happen before." A thought struck him. "Eh . . . who's goin' to move her out o' there? I mean—"

"Our people will do it." Thane gave him a cigarette and a light.

"Ta." The driver drew on the smoke with some relief. "Not as if we're paid for that, is it? An' believe me, those crushers can be dam' awkward baskets once they get jammed."

"I'll take your word for it," said Thane flatly.

So far, two patrol cars had arrived and their crews were keeping back the curious. They couldn't do anything about the tenement windows, however, and every one was opened, jammed with inquisitive spectators. One or two had cameras and were taking pictures.

Anna Marshton's blond neighbour had identified the body, then almost fainted. Now she was talking to Sandra and Francey Dunbar, standing a few feet away and keeping her back to the truck.

Thane turned to the driver again. "Is this your regular run?"

"Harald Street gets done Tuesdays an' Fridays, pal. You could set your watch by us, right?" The driver drew on his cigarette again and scowled at the crowded windows above. "Not that we get any bloody thanks from them, believe me. An' as for the muck they throw out—"

The man was still grumbling as Thane left him, walking across to where Francey Dunbar was waiting. The young black-haired sergeant was frowning intently at the high rise of the tenement's back wall.

"What's so interesting?" demanded Thane.

"This." Dunbar gestured vaguely. "It doesn't make sense."

"Explain," said Thane impatiently.

"I'll try." Dunbar frowned up at the building again. "That's the Marshton woman's window up there, right?"

Thane nodded. It was easy to locate, one of the few which didn't have at least one spectator peering down.

"Then how did her body get down here? How did it get into the rubbish skip?"

"We don't know where she was killed," Thane told him wearily. "Not yet."

"But the odds are it was in her flat," persisted Dunbar. "I was wondering"—he hesitated—"well, suppose the killer just shoved her body out of the window. Then he came down and—" His voice died away under Thane's gaze. "Not very good, is it?"

"No." Thane prodded the soft mud of the backyard with the toe of his shoe. Even the warmth of the sun still hadn't dried it out. "Not unless you show me a dent in this stuff that looks like a bomb crater," he added. "And forget the rubbish chute. It's too narrow."

"I know. I checked." Dunbar managed a sheepish attempt at a grin, then sucked the edge of his straggle of moustache. He wasn't finished. "But if she was killed up there, why dump her down here?"

"How the hell should *I* know?" countered Thane. It was just one of the puzzles in his own mind. "Panic maybe—or trying to gain time."

"If he brought her down those stairs, he took a damned big gamble," persisted Dunbar.

"He?" Thane raised an eyebrow. "Don't even say that yet."

He wasn't so sure it would have been particularly risky, not if it had been done late at night. He'd worked too many areas like Harald Street, where sensible citizens locked their doors after dark and tried hard to ignore anything short of a war that might be happening outside.

Theories could keep. For the moment, what was needed was the cold, regular routine of a murder investigation. The Divisional C.I.D. team and the usual forensic backup crew would be on their way. Anna Marshton's death, as such, belonged to them. At best, they weren't going to be overjoyed that a Crime Squad team had been roaming her flat or that the dead woman had been a potential lead in a Squad target operation.

"There's another possibility," mused Francey Dunbar. "Why she was dumped that way, I mean."

"Well?"

"Somebody just didn't like her," said Dunbar.

Thane stared at him. Francey Dunbar was serious. And, thought Thane, he might even be right.

"Maybe." Thane glanced at his watch. "I'm leaving. Get hold of Sandra. When the Divisional mob arrive, don't get in their way. But make sure you hear anything they come up with. If they start grilling you about Anna Marshton, tell them to contact Commander Hart."

Francey Dunbar nodded. "Where will you be?"

"Trying for better luck," Thane told him bitterly. "I've got to talk with a coffin-maker."

He strode away, past the garbage truck and its grim load, out through the tenement's graffiti, past the uniformed constable guarding the close mouth, and across the street to his car.

The paintwork on one door of the Ford had been scraped and gouged. A bent nail lay in the gutter beside it. He swore at the world in general, got behind the wheel, and set the car moving.

The name sounded promising, but Glenan Gardens was just a shabby little street on the west side of Glasgow. One not quite into the West End sector which was old but fashionable and where people drank homemade sherry-type wine and ate Chinese take-away meals. Instead, Glenan Gardens lay like a No Man's Land between them and the bingo halls, the bars, and the families who worried about whether there would be a pay packet next Friday or if something would ever be done about the smell from the drains.

Eventually Glenan Gardens would be demolished. It was wanted as a supermarket site. But for the moment it survived. A few of its big old houses were occupied by students who painted the doors in bright colours and lived there because the rent was cheap. The rest had become small workshops or anonymous warehouses where not everything that happened was always known to Her Majesty's inspectors of taxes.

It was years since Colin Thane had come that way, but little seemed to have changed. He parked the Ford at the kerb outside what had once been a house but now had a board above the front door which said MALDAR WOOD PRODUCTS.

The door wasn't locked. When Thane opened it and went in, the scent of fresh-cut wood was in the air, and a few steps down a drab hallway took him straight to the main workshop.

There were coffins everywhere. Coffins in all stages of construction, from newly-cut sections to completed products drying between coats of varnish. Further back, where one of the original internal walls had been knocked away, more of them lay stacked almost to the ceiling.

But it was lunch-break time. Three overalled figures were sitting at one half-finished coffin which rested on trestles, using it as a table for their tea flasks and sandwiches. One, a boy in his teens with carrot-red hair, saw Thane and nudged the fat, moon-faced man who sat next to him. The man looked round, his eyes widened, then he rose quickly and came over.

"You're a surprise, Mr. Thane!" Malky Darvel, proprietor, charge-hand and anything else necessary at Maldar Wood Products, was middle-aged and had a last few strands of hair carefully greased down across his otherwise bald head. Though his little finger was missing, the result of a onetime careless moment with a bandsaw, he gave Thane an enthusiastic pumping handshake, then stood back. "Put on weight, haven't you?"

"You mean it shows?" Thane grinned but automatically tightened his stomach muscles. "Old Man Time, Malky. It's been a few years."

"Four years next month. I'm not likely to forget."

When Colin Thane had arrested Darvel on an arson charge it had been because all the evidence pointed that way. Except that something just hadn't seemed right, had built up to a nagging doubt. Enough of a doubt to put Thane back to digging into the case. Eventually he'd pulled in Darvel's brother-in-law and had bluffed a confession out of him.

As Malky Darvel had said at the time, a man could choose his friends but not his relatives—particularly the crew he acquired by marriage.

"The word is you got promoted." Darvel eyed Thane with a slight suspicion. "We don't get many visitors—in our game customers don't exactly drop in an' ask for a fitting. So?"

"I've a problem. I think maybe you could help, Malky." Thane caught another glimpse of the youngster with the carrot-red hair, and a memory stirred. "Making it a family business now?"

"That's right." Darvel glanced back and grinned. "My son Andy—seventeen last birthday. I brought him straight in from school to learn the trade."

"Coffin-making, or your other interest?" asked Thane.

"The antiques caper?" Darvel shrugged. "Maybe later, when he's older—we'll see. But coffin-making is a good enough start-point, even though it's not the trade it used to be."

Thane raised an eyebrow. "People keep dying, don't they?"

"As far as I know." Darvel wasn't amused. His moon face shaped a scowl. "Cremation's the killer, Mr. Thane. I mean, who the hell wants craftsmanship in a casket or worries too much about style an' finish when it's for burning? It's all cost per unit, production-line stuff for them." He thumbed to where his son and the other man were drinking tea and gossiping. "Old Fred over there is one of the best coffin-makers in the business. Some of the jobs I give him I start with an apology."

"But there's your other line," murmured Thane. He met Darvel's gaze and nodded. "That's why I'm here."

"I guessed that. All right, but remember I'm not breakin' any laws." Darvel left him for a moment, murmured briefly to his son and the other man, then came back taking a bunch of keys out of a pocket. Beckoning Thane to follow, he led the way behind a stack of cut planks and unlocked a door. The room beyond was in darkness, the window tightly shuttered, but he switched on a neon tube light, then waved Thane in.

"All pretty average," he said apologetically, closing the door behind him. "I could have shown you some better stuff last month."

Several pieces of old, mostly large and heavy furniture were ranged along one wall. Some were partly dismantled. Opposite them, in various stages of construction, sat a number of smaller pieces. In between was a large workbench and a fully laden tool rack.

"That's Queen Anne." Darvel nodded towards a battered chest of drawers, almost completely taken to bits. "I've got a wee problem with it until I get hold o' some old glass. Most of the rest is Victorian rubbish—except that wardrobe. It's Sheraton." He gave Thane an impish wink. "It's what we call 'naughty'—but it's legal, remember that."

"I remember," said Thane sourly. "It's still a racket."

"But I've a happy bank manager," said Darvel without a blush. "Hell, it's not as if they were fakes, is it? That's criminal, building new pieces then conning some idiot into thinking they're old. People get hurt that way—right?" His moon face beamed. "But not with me. Anyone wi' my stuff has simply got his antiques made to measure."

The logic had a twist somewhere, but Thane decided not to get involved. Walking slowly round the little room, he inspected the mixed collection of pieces lined along the walls.

Malky Darvel was, without doubt, a craftsman. Originally, he'd been a skilled cabinetmaker. Then he'd ventured into more profitable territory—new antiques for old.

Give him something like an antique chest of drawers, too big for any modern house, and he'd convert it into two smaller chests—or an expensive kneehole desk. A wardrobe could become a bookcase, with enough left over to create something else. A fourposter bed could end up as rare candlestands and maybe a couple of tables.

If you took an antique apart and put it together again in different ways, did it stop being an antique? If even the nails, the hinges, the brass handles were period and one unpopular, low-price piece became two high-cost items, maybe the sly description "naughty" was totally right.

He glanced at the tool bench. Four years ago, Malky Darvel had told him a lot about how it was done. The cabinetmaker concerned had to know how timber was sawn in, say, the eighteenth century. Have the tools to duplicate that and the other old-fashioned techniques, resist the temptation to use modern shortcut methods.

True, not all the materials would come from genuine Chippendale, Hepplewhite or whatever. Ordinary old pieces, bought for a song in a secondhand junk shop, often played their part in the rebirth of an antique. Malky Darvel tended to slide quickly over that aspect.

Then, at the end of the day . . . Thane rubbed his hand along the smooth surface of a "new" bachelor chest, not knowing it had once been a bureau drawer and the top of a walnut card table.

The part that made it legal was the way the stuff was sold. One or two pieces, never more, would be installed in a friend's home. A telephone call from there would bring either a dealer or a salesroom expert visiting. Were they interested in buying?

No claim that the furniture was antique, valuable or anything else.

That was left to the expert.

Who took one look, gulped, took a second look and was hooked. Usually he bought, at a price where he still reckoned he was getting a bargain. Or he suggested adding the pieces to his next catalogue, on a commission basis.

When the expert sold, he labelled the pieces genuine—hell, that was why he'd bought them. From that moment they were accepted antiques, growing more respectable each time they changed hands.

With only the man who had remade them knowing better.

"You said you'd a problem, Mr. Thane," prompted Malky Darvel, who'd been watching him. "Something you're working on? If I can help, I owe you one."

"Stolen antiques—a lot of them." Thane leaned his knuckles against the workbench. "You've got the contacts, Malky. What have you heard?"

"Not a lot." The man sucked his teeth uneasily. "That's not my scene, never has been."

"But you know people," prompted Thane.

"A few." Darvel flickered a grin.

"So what's happening?"

"Among the regulars?" Darvel shrugged. "There were two for-eign teams working the East Coast a few weeks back—one Dutch, one German. Sometimes they bought, sometimes they grabbed. That's the way they operate." He frowned. "The Brighton mob haven't shown yet—it's too early for them."

Thane nodded. "The Brighton mob" was a label which cov-ered a minor swarm of smooth operators who migrated up from the south of England each summer. They worked in pairs, they were more door-to-door con men, and their ideal prey seldom came much bigger than an easily confused old woman who owned a grandfather clock or some Victorian jewellery.

"What else?" he persisted.

"Well—" The man hesitated. "There's always gossip, Mr. Thane."

"Some of it about a new team, home-grown?" demanded Thane. He shoved back from the workbench as Darvel stayed si-lent. "Malky, you said you owed me."

"And now you're debt-collecting." Darvel nodded wryly. "A few people would like to know more about them, believe me. They're smart, that's sure—and they seem to have their own con-nections. They don't unload on any of the usual dealers." He paused and shrugged. "There's a feeling they work out of Edin-burgh. Seems one of the away team from Dutchland ran foul of them there and was taken home on a stretcher. Hard men, Mr. Thane—real trouble, whoever they are."

"They're trouble," agreed Thane softly. "And maybe getting worse." He eyed Darvel. "Helping me, you could be doing some of your friends a favour."

"Or end up in one o' my own coffins, with my wife fool enough to buy retail," said Malky Darvel. He ran a careful hand over the bald dome of his head, smoothing the strands of hair, frowning. "What about afterwards? I wouldn't go in any witness box, would I?"

"You wouldn't exist," assured Thane.

"If I did, it wouldn't be for long." Darvel turned away, considered the Sheraton wardrobe's dark mahogany, then tapped the Queen Anne chest of drawers with his foot. "I'm reckoning on getting a good glass-fronted bookcase out o' this. They're in demand. Uh—I told you glass was a problem, didn't I?"

"Yes."

"The glass has to be the right age." Drawing a deep breath, Darvel faced him again. "Like out of old picture frames, Mr. Thane. Best place I know to buy picture frames cheap is in Edinburgh. How would it do if I took a trip through tomorrow?"

"Tomorrow would be fine," said Thane softly. "And once you've got your—glass?"

"You'll hear." Darvel led the way towards the door. "I reckon I know where to look."

CHAPTER 3

The sun was still drying out the city. People looked happier, dogs were finding lampposts interesting again.

And Colin Thane felt hungry. Driving away from the coffin workshop, he realised it had been a long time since breakfast. Stopping the Ford at a service station which had a transport cafe tacked on at one side, he ate a cheese sandwich and drank a cup of coffee. The tables were busy and, as he finished, a middle-aged woman, who had to be someone's mother, appeared working her way round them with a box of Ransom Trust flags and a collecting can. She saw the flag in Thane's lapel, smiled and moved on.

Thane paid his bill and got up to leave. Then a thought struck him. The woman flag-seller was still finishing her round, and he walked over to her.

"How's the money coming in?" he asked.

"Pretty well." She hefted the collecting can and it gave a heavy rattle. "So far I'm having a good day."

"When did the campaign begin?" he asked.

"In Glasgow?" She broke off to thank a truck driver who stuffed some change into her can as he went out, then beamed as she turned to Thane again. "Yesterday. It'll run all week."

"Yesterday?" Thane tried to keep his manner casual. "I thought it was earlier."

"Not in Glasgow," she said firmly. "Edinburgh's turn was last week—they did well, but we're planning to do better." She chuckled. "I mean, if Glasgow can't beat Edinburgh—"

He nodded, his mind on the Ransom Trust flag which he'd seen on Anna Marshton's coat.

"I was in Edinburgh last week," he lied. "Then I got caught again today. That's why I was curious. Was it just Edinburgh last week?"

"I think so," she said vaguely. "I don't really know much about it. I've a friend whose boy wouldn't be alive today if it hadn't been for those Ransom Trust people. That's how I got roped in."

He thanked her, put a couple of coins in the collecting can as an afterthought, and went out to his car.

He should have realised Edinburgh would come into it again. Thane sat in the Ford for a moment, frowning, knowing the charity flag on its own wasn't enough. But it could mean that Anna Marshton had gone through to the capital on the Sunday after the two local plainclothesmen had visited her.

Why? Because that was where she hoped to collect some easy money?

He shook his head and set the car moving, starting back towards the Crime Squad headquarters. After about a mile, he took a slip road which joined the southbound M.8, and as the car neared the Kingston Bridge he took an instinctive glance at one stretch of tarmac.

Half of Glasgow believed there was a body buried on that stretch, dumped while the motorway had been under construction. The legend had begun after the fourth man of a bank holdup team had quarrelled with his mates. He'd never been seen again.

It would have cost a fortune to roll back the motorway carpet. Consensus opinion was prepared to wait and see if a surprise pothole appeared someday.

Which was realistic. Thane caught the wisping thought and nodded to himself. He'd have to stay realistic on this one. Commander Hart had called it plain thief-catching. Now it was thief-catching and murder. Antiques and High Court judges. All the rest were incidental trimmings.

It was 3 P.M. when he drove in past the Police Training Area sign. In the field beside the carpark a squad of rookie mounties were busy finding out that a horse had a leg at each corner, and the inevitable sergeant was screaming at them. The rookie on the tallest horse was a girl—things were usually arranged that way.

He grinned at the sight and walked into the Crime Squad building. Maggie Fyffe was at her desk and signalled him over.

"Having a nice day?" she asked.

"No." He leaned on the counter between them. "Any more funnies like that and you can pick a window—you're leaving."

She laughed, with an edge of sympathy. "You win some, lose some. Commander Hart is out at a committee meeting. You've to stay till he gets back."

"He knows?"

She nodded. "And Francey Dunbar called in. The Divisional man on the murder is a Detective Chief Inspector Kiesen."

"I know him." Thane couldn't put much enthusiasm into the words. He'd had to work with Fred Kiesen at Divisional level, and neither had enjoyed it. Kiesen was a dour, by-the-book individual, nearing retirement age. Any enthusiasm he had left was reserved for calculating his pension rights. "Any good news for me—for a change?"

"Not today," she said. "Superintendent, if you want to moan about life, call your wife. It's her job to listen, not mine—anyway, she phoned looking for you."

"Get back on your broomstick," he said wearily and turned away.

He didn't see the look of understanding in Maggie Fyffe's eyes as she watched him go. For reasons that went beyond being a cop's widow, Maggie Fyffe was unreservedly devoted to what she considered "her" men on the Crime Squad. It was incidental that she would have died before letting them realise it.

Tie loosened, jacket off, Colin Thane lifted the telephone and dialled his home number as soon as he was in his office and behind his desk.

The number rang out and was answered quickly by a young

voice. He grinned. Daughters aged eleven seemed to regard telephones as personal property.

"Me, Kate," he said.

"Hello, Dad." She sounded slightly disappointed. "Mum's out.
I thought you were Judy."

"I'm not." Judy was Kate's school friend and had the same attitude to telephones. He glanced at his watch. "What happened
to school?"

"Half day for a teachers' meeting," his daughter answered
nonchalantly. "Judy thinks they're going on strike."

"Good," he said absently. "What about Tommy?"

"His too." She preferred verbal shorthand. "He took off somewhere."

He pursed his lips. Tommy was thirteen now, beginning to
show signs of preferring his own way. That, and something more
—an at times almost aggressive silence. Thane knew he was
going to have to talk to him, talk to him properly, without being
totally certain why.

"Did Mum leave a message for me?" he asked.

"I've to tell you Uncle Phil phoned. He's coming over tonight."
His daughter's voice held a touch of impatience. "Dad, I'm expecting Judy to call."

"Sorry," said Thane meekly.

He hung up, eyed the red cover of the robberies file lying
where he'd placed it on the desk, and resisted the temptation to
light a cigarette.

It was a month or so since he'd seen Phil Moss. For years,
Moss had been his second-in-command at Millside Division, but
when the partnership had been broken Moss had first gone into
hospital for an overdue stomach ulcer operation, then had been
moved into a partly administrative job at Strathclyde headquarters.

He still missed having Moss at his side. He wasn't sure if he'd
ever get quite the same relationship with Francey Dunbar. But if
Moss was coming round, he made a mental note to collect a bottle on his way home.

Meantime . . . lifting the receiver again, he dialled the direct-line number for the Crime Squad unit office in Edinburgh. In another moment he was talking to the duty officer there.

"What do you know about a Dutch team working antiques over your way?" asked Thane.

"I've heard of them, sir," confirmed the duty officer. "We weren't involved, but the local forces were chasing them."

"*Were?*" asked Thane.

"They've been and gone," explained the man. "That's how they work, sir—a week or so of hard thieving, then straight back to Holland till next time."

"They don't hang about?"

"The Edinburgh cops label them 'The Flying Dutchmen,'" said the duty officer wryly. "They use an advance man who sets up the jobs for them—he scouts cottage-in-the-country stuff, old ladies up to their necks in Ming vases."

Thane could guess the rest. The main team moving in, half a dozen village cops suddenly with break-ins on their hands and on a loser from the start.

"Then there's the Afrika Korps," volunteered the Edinburgh man helpfully. "A German mob, on the same game."

"I'd heard." So far, everything Malky Darvel had told him seemed to check out. The fat-faced little coffin-maker's contacts were as good as ever. Thane sucked his teeth. "I've been tipped one of the Dutch visitors was roughed up in your territory. He could have needed hospital treatment."

"I'll check," promised the duty officer. He hesitated. "Uh—Commander Hart had us digging out crime reports, sir. He seemed to think there was a new antiques team at work, home-grown."

"That's right," said Thane.

"The Dutch and the Germans haven't pulled anything really big I know about." The duty officer sounded worried. "If there is a new outfit, they haven't pulled a job in Edinburgh yet."

"That's interesting, isn't it," said Thane neutrally. "Get back to me."

He hung up again. The man was right. It had been nagging at the back of his mind without Thane being able to grasp it. Edinburgh had been immune as far as the robberies file list was concerned. Maybe the antiques team didn't believe in working too close to home.

There was one more call he wanted to make. The Ransom Trust had no listing in the Glasgow telephone directory, but he found an office number in the Edinburgh book. But as he reached for the telephone his door opened and Francey Dunbar ambled in.

"How was Chief Inspector Kiesen?" asked Thane dryly.

"Not exactly friendly, sir." Dunbar said it stonily and closed the door behind him with a gentle heel tap.

"So?"

"We kept out of his way." Dunbar scratched his thin straggle of moustache. "There's a Mrs. Mulholland next close along— widowed, in her seventies, lives at her window."

"There always is," said Thane gravely.

"She's good." Dunbar grimaced appreciatively. "Two men she decided were C.I.D. visited Harald Street on Sunday afternoon."

"They were," nodded Thane. "They talked to Anna Marshton."

"I see." Dunbar blinked. "I've still to read that file. Anyway, about an hour after they left, a taxi arrived. Anna Marshton got in and it drove off. Another taxi brought her back in the early evening." He looked disappointed at Thane's lack of reaction. "She must have been away about five hours."

"You told Kiesen?" asked Thane.

"Yes, but he didn't seem interested," said Dunbar. "Sandra came back with me. She's trying to get a line on the taxi situation. If the Marshton woman ordered the first one by phone, the call should be logged—"

"Tell Sandra it could be into town, then a train for Edinburgh." He explained about the charity flag, saw Dunbar's eyes widen with interest, and added, "The return taxi could be from the station rank. Try it anyway."

Dunbar nodded. "There's—well, something later, sir. Kiesen likes it."

"Chief Inspector Kiesen," corrected Thane. "Well?"

"Two teenagers who were necking in that shop doorway across the street—Ma Mulholland saw them, and they're local." Dunbar shuffled his feet a little. "The girl's name is Betty Campbell—the family are the original Orange Protestant fanatics. Her boyfriend is Irish Catholic, so she can't take him home—"

"Francey." Thane stopped him with a scowl. "This better have a middle and end. It's a hell of a long beginning."

"We found them," said Dunbar, unimpressed. "The girl knows Anna Marshton. Says she left home about eleven on Sunday night. Straight away a car drew up, Anna got into it, and it drove past their doorway—the girl says another woman was driving it."

Thane stiffened. "What else have you got?"

"Not a hell of a lot," admitted Dunbar. "The woman looked young, long dark hair—probably brunette. She can't remember the car, and her boyfriend just thinks it was a Fiat." He shrugged. "Ma Mulholland was off duty—she watches late-night TV religion."

"Like you said, you haven't seen the file," Thane said. "A long-haired brunette eased a load of antique furniture past a traffic cop the day after Bloody Mac's place was done."

"Christ," said Francey Dunbar with feeling. He swallowed hard. "But Anna Marshton got home again, didn't she? Or—"

"Or it was meant to look that way," said Thane. "What was she wearing when the Campbell girl saw her?"

"No coat, a jacket—just as we found her."

"Carrying a handbag?"

"Yes." His sergeant's thin young face showed uncertainty. "Her handbag was in the house, wasn't it?"

"Handbag and keys—unless Kiesen found others in among that garbage." Dunbar's silence was answer enough. Thane got to his feet and picked up the file. "We don't know where she was killed, Francey. Maybe it doesn't matter. But someone went back to her place, went back to look it over—to make sure there was nothing embarrassing lying around."

They went through together to the duty room and gathered up Sandra Craig and Joe Felix. Felix was balding, in his mid-thirties, and stockily built. His desk, which they used as a conference table, was a litter of electronic components. Some were Crime Squad, others looked suspiciously like the insides of a couple of domestic cassette players. When he wasn't working, Detective Constable Felix ran a small sideline in mending colleagues' home audio gear.

The few other Crime Squad officers in the duty room gave an occasional glance in their direction, but otherwise left them alone as Thane got down to giving all three a detailed briefing. He held nothing back, partly because he knew that if he did they'd make a point of finding out anyway.

"Comment?" he asked as he finished.

"Your coffin-maker, sir." Felix rubbed his chin thoughtfully. "Does he know about the Marshton woman being killed?"

"No."

"We're—uh—dropping him in it, then?"

"We need him," said Thane. "He's cautious by nature."

Felix glanced at Sandra and Dunbar. They said nothing, and he shrugged.

"I could fit him with a radio bug," he suggested.

"He'll be happier on his own." Thane sensed their disapproval, but he knew Malky Darvel. He saw Sandra frown but stopped the redhead. "That's how it is."

It was several more minutes before he left them. Each of the three had a list of immediate areas. Each was going to be tied to a desk and a telephone for some time. He left Sandra Craig tackling the Anna Marshton side, but Sergeant Dunbar and Felix drew what Thane mentally labelled "ground clearance" on the robbery file's listings, from the overall insurance cover picture to, in Felix's case, an assessment of the security systems installed.

Dull and routine—but that kind of dull routine every now and again threw up its own surprise.

Back in his own office, he found a telex message lying on his desk. It was from the Crime Squad office in Edinburgh.

HANS RUDOLPH SCHILTON, NETHERLANDS NATIONAL, AGE THIRTY, TREATED HOSPITAL HERE LAST MONTH. BROKEN ARM, CONCUSSION, MULTIPLE ABRASIONS. CLAIMED MUGGING VICTIM, UNSUBSTANTIATED. SELF-DISCHARGED HOSPITAL AFTER THREE DAYS. UNDERSTOOD RETURNED NETHERLANDS ON DISCHARGE.

Malky Darvel's batting average was staying high. He marked the telex for Francey Dunbar and was setting it aside when the telephone rang. He answered it.

"We met earlier today, Superintendent," said a man's voice, brisk and confident. "Peter Barry—it was when you were with Lord Mackenzie."

"I remember." Thane blinked, surprised. About the next thing he'd intended doing was check on the Ransom Trust flag-selling situation. "In fact, I—"

"He told me about you," said Barry without letting him finish. "Are you going to be at his place tomorrow?"

"That's what he wants," agreed Thane cautiously.

"Then my sister Shona would like to speak to you," said Barry cheerfully. "Here she is."

There was a moment's pause, then she came on the line, a shyer, slightly hesitant voice.

"It's about tomorrow, Superintendent. I'm secretary of the Ransom Trust, and we have this committee meeting at Drum Lodge—anyway, I wondered if you could help us."

"Help?" queried Thane. "How?"

"Advice," she explained. "The Trust is planning an antiques fair—a touring fund-raising exhibition. The way things are, we're worried about security."

"I'm no antiques expert," Thane told her dryly.

"We've plenty of *them.*" She gave a slight chuckle. "Maybe too many. But you'll be at Drum Lodge. If you could stay on for the meeting, talk to some of us—"

"Sorry," said Thane firmly. Accepting that kind of invitation could have led to a demarcation war inside any force. "It's not my area. But I can get you a good Crime Prevention officer—that's how he earns his keep."

"That would help," she said resignedly. "Sorry to trouble you."

"I'll fix it," promised Thane. Then he added, "Your collectors are working hard through here—you probably heard that from your brother. When did the Edinburgh collection end?"

"Sunday," Shona Barry told him without hesitation. "They made their target, and more."

"Was it just Edinburgh last week?"

"Yes." She laughed. "Each district committee picks its own week. Glasgow and Edinburgh always have a battle to see who gets in first."

Thane said goodbye and hung up.

He'd confirmed what he wanted. The rest almost amused him. Whether he liked it or not, he was gradually becoming entangled in the antiques game. The only surprise was that Bloody Mac seemed to have given Peter Barry a heavy hint at what was happening—which didn't say too much for the discretion of one of Her Majesty's judges.

Maggie Fyffe was best placed to make the Crime Prevention arrangement. He scribbled a note for her, then changed his mind and took it through himself. As he'd hoped, he'd timed it well. She'd made a fresh pot of coffee.

Jack Hart arrived back at five. Minutes later, Thane had been summoned through.

"I've had a bad afternoon," said Hart grimly. "I've fought off penny-pinching civil servants who want economies and thick-skulled politicians who want miracles." He sat back, closing his eyes, his thin, lined face tired. "All right, Anna Marshton—give me the basics."

Thane did, trimming down to essentials. Eyes still closed, the Squad commander listened in silence, apart from an occasional grunt. At the finish he opened his eyes and leaned forward.

"So you'd gamble she went to Edinburgh?"

Thane nodded. Sandra Craig had traced the first taxi. It had taken the dead woman direct to Queen Street Station, where the Glasgow–Edinburgh rail service operated. The taxi which had brought her home had come from the station rank a few hours later.

"It almost helps," said Hart with a degree of satisfaction.

"Sir?" Thane shifted in his seat, puzzled.

"Diplomacy," explained the Squad commander patiently. "Fred Kiesen has the murder inquiry and he's an awkward bastard, right?"

"Mostly." Thane waited.

"I spoke to some of your old bosses at Strathclyde." Hart closed his eyes again. "We worked out an operational deal. Kiesen keeps the murder as a Divisional case, you stay on your side of the fence and stick with the robberies." He made a noise which could have been a chuckle. "You cooperate, of course, where there's overlap—and Anna Marshton is still part of the robbery package, from our viewpoint."

"Does Kiesen know?" To Thane, the "operational deal" sounded more like a suitably hazy piece of police politics.

"Enough to keep him happy," said Hart. "But go and see him. Make a few soothing noises. It's a small price."

He saw Francey Dunbar first, told him the team could call it a day, and that they'd see how things stood by morning. Then, after clearing his desk, he left the building, got back into his car, and set off again for Harald Street.

It was a slower journey, the city's rush-hour close to its peak. Moving with the flow, the dusty Crime Squad car just one more anonymous vehicle in the home-going traffic, he thought ahead and knew talking to Chief Inspector Kiesen wasn't going to be easy.

But at least Commander Hart had smoothed the way. Hart usually could—whether it was an administrative tangle or a committee battle.

Watching the car in front, easing his accelerator as it slowed, Thane shook his head. Jack Hart was still a good cop, but had become an administrator. If that fate ever came his own way, he doubted how he would cope.

He trickled the Ford on, frowning, then found it easier to think of Harald Street.

A lot easier. Colin Thane knew the Harald Streets, how they ticked and why, and had his own brand of sympathy for the ordinary men and women trapped in them.

They'd been planned and built so that the old festering Glasgow slums could be demolished. But he'd never met a planner who had spent even one night in a Harald Street.

Planners planned, people had to live with the results—and having to exist in a high-rise jungle like Harald Street wasn't easy. Not when it came to trying to stick wallpaper on walls that dribbled condensation while ceilings grew black mould, because the planners had built in heating systems too expensive for the average tenant to run. Not when social amenities meant a few scattered shops with metal grilles over the windows and steel shutters on the doors. Not when a teenager could only hang around a street corner—or when having to give your home address wiped out the chance of getting a decent job.

The Harald Streets, the already grubby filing cabinets for people, might have better plumbing than the old slums. But that apart, they showed every sign of becoming worse than what they'd replaced.

The thought stayed with him the rest of the way until he turned into Harald Street. A few early drunks were in sight, the usual scavenging dogs ran along the pavements, and some older children were trying to dismantle an abandoned van. But the women who leaned out of their open windows were more interested in the free show down the road—the big Command Unit vehicle lying outside Anna Marshton's close mouth.

Thane stopped near it, got out, and walked across past the other police cars parked around. The Command Unit, a mobile office and communications base built on a truck chassis, had a uniformed constable on guard at its rear door.

Climbing the steps, nodding to the constable, Thane went in. A detective glanced up from a desk where he was tapping a typewriter, recognised him, and started to rise.

"Don't bother." Thane waved him down. "Where's your boss?"

"Through the back, sir." The man gestured towards a door in a partition wall, and smothered a grin. "He—uh—"

"Hoped I'd look in?" suggested Thane.

Crossing over, he opened the door and stepped into the tiny office beyond. It had a built-in desk and bench seating, but Detective Chief Inspector Kiesen, a burly, balding man with grey hair, was standing scowling at a street map he'd pinned to one wall.

"Hello, Fred," said Thane, closing the door behind him.

"You got round to it, did you?" Kiesen faced him and glared. An ill-fitting blue serge suit, white shirt and black tie, his usual dress, gave him the air of a professional mourner, and his voice was an odd, menacing hiss—always had been, since he'd been kicked in the throat when a beat cop. The unkind suggested that if Kiesen had been kicked on the head it would have caused less damage, though it might have meant a broken ankle for his assailant.

"All right, Fred, you're sore," said Thane. "I dumped a murder on your lap." He hoped a lie would help. "I had my own problems—then I heard you were on your way. I knew it wouldn't need both of us."

"So you just left two of your private Mafia behind, to get in the way?" Kiesen stayed belligerent, thumbs hooking into the slack waistband of his trousers. "You may have become one of the anointed, Thane—more rank and a Crime Squad job. But first you messed up that damned flat, then your sergeant and that female hijack my witnesses. Expect me to thank you?"

"Not when it's you, Fred." Thane tried to hide the sarcasm. It was easier to stay penitent. "It was a bad start. But that's been sorted out. You've heard?"

"Headquarters spelled it out," said Kiesen in his throaty rasp. He sniffed derisively. "Cooperate—so far, I don't see much need."

"You could be right," said Thane. He went over to the wall map and considered it. "Made much progress?"

"Some." Kiesen's manner became vaguely condescending. "The postmortem report won't be ready till tomorrow, but the medical estimate is time of death was between midnight Sunday and two A.M. Monday." He sucked his lips. "The forensic mob have finished and gone back to their tea and microscopes. I've got most of my boys working door-to-door along the street—not that it's doing much good. Your average punter is doing a three-wise-monkeys act—saw nothing, heard nothing, knows nothing."

"Any personal hunch?" asked Thane.

"I stick to facts," said Kiesen.

"Of course." Thane nodded encouragingly. "Still, with your experience—"

"Facts," said Kiesen flatly, then gave way to temptation. "But I don't buy a link between your interest and murder."

"Facts?" asked Thane.

Kiesen sniffed. "She took off on the Sunday night, right?"

"Late on," agreed Thane. "Two witnesses—the pair my sergeant passed to you."

"Correct." Kiesen flushed at the reminder. "The word is Anna Marshton was on the game, part-time. So another of them collects her that night and they go into the city, looking for business. Anna picks up a punter, brings him home—and he shapes as a grade-one headbanger." He gestured brutally. "Goodbye, Anna—it happens often enough."

Thane stared at him. "You really see it like that?"

"A plain, ordinary headbanger," insisted Kiesen. "Who else would bother lugging her down to that rubbish skip?"

"I didn't see any sign of a struggle up there," said Thane.

"Then he's a tidy headbanger," said Kiesen.

"You could be right." Thane saw no point in arguing, and kept a grim hold on his patience. "But try it on me again when you've got the other woman who was in that car."

"Right." Kiesen grinned at him. "I will, Superintendent. Till then, you've your own little worries. Leave this one to the working cops, that's my advice."

"I'll be in touch, Fred," said Thane quietly, clinging to the last remains of his self-control.

Turning, he went out. The detective at the typewriter suddenly made himself busy and stayed that way until Thane had left the Command Unit. The Unit's partitioning was anything but soundproof, he'd heard most of it—and the rest of the Divisional team would be more than interested.

Even if most of them thought Kiesen was an idiot.

Colin Thane got back into his car, allowed himself the safety-valve luxury of slamming a fist hard in anger against the steering wheel, then keyed the starter. He reversed clear of the other police cars, then drove away from the Command Unit vehicle, still feeling partly stunned at Kiesen's attitude.

He took a right turn at the next corner, heading back towards the city. The Ford swung into a shabby side street, waste ground on one side, a deserted school building on the other. That barely registered as he swore aloud, staring ahead.

A girl in a summer dress was struggling to get free from three men. They were at the pavement's edge, almost at the school gates. One man had her by the hair, another was trying to rip her shoulder bag from her grasp. As Thane's foot went down hard on the accelerator, the third attacker hit the girl with his fist and she went down.

They heard the car coming. One thug kicked the girl where she lay and grabbed the bag. He had fair hair and, like the others, he was young, dressed in denims and sweatshirt, and had been taken totally by surprise. As Thane skidded the car to a halt beside them and jumped out, they hesitated.

"Take him," urged one, face twisting in a savage grin. His hand dropped to the heavy leather belt at his waist and came up again holding a short broad-bladed knife. "Do the bampot in— come on!"

His companions still hesitated. Thane didn't. Charging forward, he dodged a slicing swing of the young thug's knife arm, grabbed his wrist, and simultaneously kicked him hard in the crotch. The scream of pain as the thug folded became a gurgle as Thane chopped him behind the ear with the edge of his free hand.

The knife clattering from his grip, he slumped to the pavement. Thane swung round, and the other two started running, out across the street, heading for the waste ground. The fair-haired man still had the girl's shoulder bag.

Sprinting after them, Thane closed the gap on the bag-snatcher, then took him in a diving tackle. They went down together, then the fair-haired figure abandoned the shoulder bag, scrambled free, and took off again. By the time Thane was on his feet, both figures had reached the houses on the far side of the waste ground and had disappeared up an entry.

Dusting himself down, collecting the shoulder bag, he gave up and returned to the school gates. The thug he'd knocked down had vanished, though his knife still lay glinting on the tarmac. The attacked girl was on her feet, looking dazed, leaning against the gateway.

"How do you feel?" asked Thane.

"I'll manage, mister." She was dark-haired, reasonably pretty, and looked about seventeen. A red patch below one eye would be a bruise by morning, and she was pressing her side where she'd been kicked. She nodded her thanks as Thane gave her the shoulder bag. "You're a cop, right?"

"Yes." Now it was over, they were no longer alone. Half a dozen people had already appeared from somewhere; others were gradually, unhurriedly joining them. He turned back to the girl. "Know who they were?"

She shook her head, but he knew she was lying.

"Recognise them again?"

"No." She met his gaze steadily. "Might as well forget it, right?"

He sighed and faced the cluster of spectators.

"Any of you see them?"

All interest suddenly blanked from their faces. A couple began to drift away. As they did, a man with a scarred face pushed forward and murmured to the girl. She listened, then turned to Thane.

"He's a friend, mister. He'll see me home. All right?"

Thane stooped, picked up the knife, then looked at her again. She smiled at him, with an understanding beyond her years. But they had their own code in Harald Street.

He nodded, turned away, and walked back to the car.

"Hey, friend." As he got in behind the wheel, the man with the scarred face came over. "What's your name?"

"Thane." He glanced over towards the girl, now surrounded by the others. "They roughed her up. She should see a doctor."

"Aye." The scarred face twisted in a grin. "She says the one you got in the slats will need a vet."

The man left him. As Thane started the Ford and set it moving, the crowd was breaking up, the girl and her escort were walking away. He watched them for a moment in the rear mirror, then shrugged and decided to forget it.

He got home after six. Home was a small, very ordinary bungalow in a suburban street where most of the houses looked and were exactly the same, give or take the odd extension or who had found the time and money for a do-it-yourself outside paint job.

Colin Thane ran the Ford into a narrow driveway which wasn't much longer than the car. Daylight was starting to fade and there were some fresh heavy clouds in the sky. Holding the bottle of whisky he'd bought at the local supermarket, he got out and locked the Ford. Three cars had been stolen in the street in the last couple of weeks, all later found abandoned but stripped of radios and anything else of value.

The house door opened as he reached it. Mary Thane greeted him with a smile and the kind of kiss that showed she still meant it.

"Booze, at least, you don't forget," she declared, seeing the bottle. "Phil said he'll be here about nine."

"Someone else must be feeding him." He followed her in.

Kate was in the front room, sprawled on a couch watching TV, school books abandoned on the carpet beside her. At her feet the brindle shape of Clyde, their boxer dog, twitched slightly and gave a token wag of his stumpy tail as Thane looked in.

He followed Mary through to the kitchen. A slim, attractive, dark-haired woman, she still wore the same dress size as when they'd married. Still wore the same dresses too, was her usual comment to that one. He grinned, watching her busy with the evening meal. Looking at her, it was hard to believe they'd soon have yet another wedding anniversary coming up.

"Where's Tommy?" he asked.

"Still out." She said it with faint edge, but made no other comment. "Better get cleaned up. Food's just about ready."

He went upstairs, washed, changed into a sport shirt and a pair of old corduroy slacks, then went back down again. As he entered the kitchen, the back door opened and Tommy came in. His son flushed as he saw them.

"You're late," said Mary.

"Sorry." He had her dark hair and a lean, sturdy build, and was in his after-school sweater and jeans. "I was at Andy Lyall's place."

"Again?" Thane frowned. Andy Lyall was a couple of years older than Tommy, lanky and spotty, the son of a couple who ran a corner grocery store. "It's getting to be a habit—that, and being late."

"I said sorry." Tommy gave a near truculent scowl. "I meant to be back."

"Make sure of it next time," said Thane more curtly than he meant. He tried again. "Look, ever think we might start worrying about what's happened?"

He didn't get an answer.

The evening meal passed peacefully enough. Afterwards, Tommy and Kate both went out. It was their youth club night.

At nine, it began to rain. Phil Moss arrived soon afterwards, complained as he dumped his dripping coat in the hallway, then settled onto his favourite seat in the front room. He fussed over Clyde for a moment; then, as the boxer subsided at his feet, he collapsed back.

"Would a drink help?" asked Thane.

"It might." Moss's thin face showed approval.

He was about ten years older than Thane, and though his scrawny frame had gained a few pounds since surgery, the rest hadn't changed too much. Moss still dressed as if his clothes came from charity handouts, was still an aggressive bachelor, and hadn't particularly mellowed his acid view on most things that went on around him.

"I heard you got yourself into a tangle with Fred Kiesen," he said dryly, watching Thane pour the drinks. He took his glass as Mary brought it over and winked at her. "Kiesen wasn't too pleased."

"I'll survive," murmured Thane. Moss's new job at Strathclyde headquarters was with the Assistant Chief Constable, Crime. He heard most things that happened. "How is Kiesen now?"

"Stamping around." Moss sipped his drink and nodded approval. "Not bad. The trouble is, I'm not supposed to drink on an empty stomach—not yet, anyway." He glanced appealingly at Mary. "I came straight from work."

They fed him, gossiped for a spell, then Mary left saying she had ironing to do. Thane poured Moss another drink, topped his own glass, then sat back.

"What else did you hear about Kiesen?" he asked.

"That he prefers the sex angle. You're staying with the antiques idea? It makes more sense."

Thane nodded.

"If you need any help, back-door style—" Moss didn't finish.

"So I don't tread directly on Kiesen's toes?" Thane knew there was more to the offer than either friendship or diplomacy. Phil Moss would still prefer to be a working cop, out on the streets. "If forensic or the autopsy report turn up anything interesting, I'd like to know."

"Right." Moss looked slightly disappointed, then switched tactics. "There was more trouble near Harald Street this evening— no connection, but interesting. Some local heavies chased three young neds and knocked hell out of them." He paused and raised an eyebrow. "Something about a girl roughed up earlier and rescued by a cop. Know anything about it?"

"Nothing that matters," said Thane.

"A pity," said Moss solemnly. Stooping, he scratched Clyde behind one ear. "This cop rates as a local hero. The girl was carrying pay-out money from the neighbourhood bookie. If she'd been robbed, it would have been sacrilege." He sank deeper into his chair, swirled the liquor in his glass, then asked bluntly, "What's your next move in the antiques job?"

Glad of a chance to use someone outside it as a sounding board, Thane told him how things stood. Listening intently, Moss gave an occasional critical grunt but still nodded a general agreement at the finish.

"When do you start working the Edinburgh end?" he demanded.

"Tomorrow," said Thane. "But I need more than I've got."

"That's a fair understatement," mused Moss. He scratched his thin chest for a moment. "If this mob sticks to pattern, there's another robbery due soon."

"Thanks," said Thane. "That's more or less what Bloody Mac told me—and that it could be bigger."

"Happy thought." Moss considered the dog at his feet for a moment, then nodded. "Yes, the old devil could be right."

Tommy and Kate returned home soon after that. They treated Moss as an uncle, but for once Tommy's greeting was unusually subdued. If Moss noticed, he said nothing, and later, once the two had been despatched to bed, Mary brought through more sandwiches and a pot of coffee.

It was close to midnight when Moss left, and the rain had died away. Yawning, Mary tidied up with Thane's help, then headed for bed.

Thane hung back. Standing in the kitchen, hearing Clyde already snoring in his basket, he saw some of Tommy's school books lying ready for the morning. Casually, he picked up the science textbook which topped the pile and flicked it open. Then his lips tightened. On the inside cover page, where Tommy had written his name, it had been scored out. Underneath, in another childish hand, someone had scrawled "Kill the Fuzz."

He closed the book, put out the light, and left the kitchen. Going along to Tommy's room, he quietly opened the door. The bedroom was in darkness, but enough light spilled in from the hall to show Tommy was asleep.

His son stirred slightly. Gently, Thane closed the door again.

Mary was reading in bed when he reached their room. He said nothing about it to her. But it stayed in his mind, and sleep didn't come easily.

CHAPTER 4

Anna Marshton's murder rated only a few lines in the next morning's newspapers. A new crisis had begun boiling in the Middle East, a TV personality was caught up in a London sex scandal, and yet another football manager featured in a "You can't fire me, I quit," row. Against that kind of opposition, no news editor could be interested in a down-market killing.

Colin Thane scanned the newspaper stories at the breakfast table while Mary hustled the children through coffee and toast and off to school. Kate left first. As Tommy followed, Thane went after him and stopped him at the front door.

"Hold on a moment." He gave his son an awkward smile and laid a friendly hand on his shoulder. "This isn't a good time to ask—I know it. But sometimes being a cop's son isn't too easy. Any problems at school?"

"No." Tommy avoided looking at him and fidgeted. "Why?"

"A notion I had." Thane drew a breath. "We could talk about it. Tonight, maybe."

"There's nothing." Tommy moistened his lips. "I'll be late. Can I go now?"

Thane nodded. As the front door banged shut, he went back through to the kitchen.

"What was that about?" asked Mary, frowning.

"It's called communication," said Thane wryly. "One-way variety."

He poured another cup of coffee and drank it gloomily while he finished the newspapers. It hadn't been much of a try and it had got him nowhere. There had to be a better way, next time.

The drive from home to the Squad headquarters building took twenty minutes and he stopped the Ford in the parking lot exactly at 9 A.M. Inside the building, Sandra Craig and Joe Felix were already waiting in his office. Tucking away a racing sheet, Felix gave him a cheerful grin. The redhead managed a nod, finished chewing an egg sandwich, and wiped her fingers on some paper tissues.

"Where's Francey?" demanded Thane.

"Still on his way." Felix stopped it there as a motorcycle came snarling into the parking lot. Through the window they saw Sergeant Dunbar abandon the machine then walk towards the building, removing his crash helmet. Felix gave a faint chuckle. "I think that's reentry. Uh—a man telephoned a few minutes ago, sir. Asked for you but wouldn't give his name."

Thane frowned. "Any message?"

Felix shook his head. "Just that he'd call back. He sounded local."

It was left there as Francey Dunbar arrived. Dumping the helmet on Thane's desk, he mumbled a greeting. He looked red-eyed and hadn't shaved.

"Late night, Sergeant?" asked Thane.

"Later than I meant." Dunbar gave a sheepish grin. "A friend arrived back in town."

"Your place or hers?" asked Sandra. She winked at Felix. "She didn't leave much for the rest of us."

Thane stopped it developing, and turned to Felix.

"Finished the security and insurance picture?"

"Nearly," said Felix cautiously. "From what's in the file and checking, there's nothing obvious. Every house robbed had a fairly good alarm system, no common layout—"

"But the robbery team still knocked them out?"

Felix nodded.

"Insurance cover?"

"Mixed." Felix glanced at Francey Dunbar and got a nod of agreement. "One or two policy updates, routine revaluation, at least two definitely underinsured and howling. No bad claims histories." He shrugged. "I've still a few ends to tie up."

"Do that, and watch the Glasgow situation—but stay clear of Kiesen." Thane switched to the girl beside him. "You'll open up the Edinburgh end, Sandra. Smile at the local cops, find out more about the Dutchman who was beaten up, anything else there is. Francey and I will meet up with you there."

She nodded calmly. "When and where, sir? If it's around lunchtime, there's a wine bar off Princes Street where the pizza is homemade."

"I know it," said Dunbar. "But the way you eat, can we afford it?" He paused, eyes widening and staring at Thane. "Wait a minute. You want me with you at Drum Lodge?"

Thane nodded. "I may need a human sacrifice."

"That's what I thought," said Dunbar bitterly, picking up his helmet. "Except that Bloody Mac doesn't eat sergeants—we're not worth it. He just chews us for flavour, then spits us out."

First off was Sandra Craig, heading her red sports-tuned Mini on the motorway route for Edinburgh. A few minutes later, after a final word with Joe Felix, Thane went out to the parking lot. Francey Dunbar was waiting beside the Ford, and Thane suppressed a smile.

Somehow in the short space of time, his sergeant had shaved and had managed to change his black roll-neck for a conservative grey shirt and dark tie. The suede jacket and the rest of Dunbar's outfit might not be what the well-dressed cop always wore, but Dunbar was trying.

"Changing your image, Francey?" he asked.

"No." Dunbar flushed a little. "Trying to help yours. Think he'll ask if we've washed?"

Thane grinned, shook his head and motioned to Dunbar to take the wheel while he slid into the passenger seat.

They set off, the car's exhaust a brisk, belligerent purr. Francey Dunbar handled any car with an ease and understanding that seemed to communicate, make it match his mood.

There were gaps in what Thane knew about him, despite his record sheet. His parents lived in a village somewhere near Edinburgh, he had his bachelor pad in Glasgow, and his motorcycle was a 750cc Honda which he had raced a few times. But go beyond that, and the ability to always find a good-looking girl willing to keep him fed, and Sergeant Dunbar kept a low off-duty profile.

Thane shrugged to himself, listening to Dunbar whistling softly between his teeth, watching the car slip through the traffic, taking the north road out of the city.

When you were a cop, a low profile was sometimes the best way to survive.

It was a ninety-minute journey, the first half by motorway route which passed the national shrine of Bannockburn, where Scots built a monument to an ancient battle against England but then took long enough raising the money to pay for it. Then on beyond the old town of Stirling and its castle and into Perthshire, the flat farming Lowlands left behind, the wooded hills and glens of the Highlands taking over in dramatic contrast.

The last part was narrow, winding roads, meeting farm trucks loaded with sheep or the occasional bulk tanker carrying whisky from the hill distilleries. Drum village came up, a thin scatter of cottages and a single hotel. Beyond it, they passed farms where hairy long-horned Highland cattle grazed in pocket-sized fields. Then they saw a sign for Drum Lodge and Francey Dunbar braked, turning off into a long driveway flanked by high, pink-flowered rhododendron bushes.

They emerged with Drum Lodge immediately ahead. In daylight, Lord Mackenzie's home was an old, modestly sized, two-storey stone house fronted by a small formal garden and a gravel parking area, which was empty. Leaving the Ford there, they crunched across the gravel towards the front door.

"Looks normal enough," muttered Dunbar, giving the house an aggressive glare.

"Dungeons are only open at weekends," Thane reassured him. "Come on."

They'd been seen. The front door opened and a buxom, grey-haired woman came out onto the porch, watching their approach with a degree of disapproval. She glanced round as Lord Mackenzie emerged from the house and joined her.

"All right, Annie," he said briskly. "I told you I'd cope with visitors—you've enough to do today."

His housekeeper went back indoors and Bloody Mac, looking more like farmer than judge in checked wool shirt, tweed trousers and brown boots, greeted Thane with a smile. He shook hands with a slightly apprehensive Dunbar and then led them through a wood-panelled hall and into his study.

"Not quite as well furnished as it used to be," he said with an acid touch of humour, indicating the bare floorboards and the empty row of glass-fronted cabinets. "Sit down, Thane. You too, Sergeant."

They took two of the chairs placed round a long table in the middle of the room. Lord Mackenzie remained standing for a moment, his sharp, bright eyes considering them each in turn.

"Should I ask what progress you've made?" he asked bluntly.

"That depends what you've heard," countered Thane.

"Heard?" Lord Mackenzie raised an eyebrow. Then he understood. "No, I told you yesterday. I'm a private citizen in this." He saw Francey Dunbar's disbelief. "That strains your credulity, Sergeant?"

"Not if you say so, sir," said Dunbar.

"I see." For a moment, the little man's face hardened and Bloody Mac took over. "You haven't made an appearance in my court, have you?"

Dunbar shook his head.

"Then that's something we can both await with interest." Manner still frosty, Mackenzie settled in a chair opposite them. "Well, Thane?"

"How much do you really know?" asked Thane.

"Very little." Mackenzie frowned. "I was told your people had

decided the antiques robberies were linked, that they had become what you term a 'target'—and that there was some positive
lead."

"It stopped being positive. But there may be others."

"May?" Mackenzie sighed and glanced at his emptied cabinets. "You wouldn't make a good salesman. I suppose you both
realise that this country is the perfect hunting ground for antiques?"

"Britain?" Francey Dunbar blinked. "What makes us special?"

"Britain in general, but Scotland in particular, Sergeant," said
Lord Mackenzie patiently. "The legitimate antiques trade has
been buying in England for generations. Scotland is territory
they're still just beginning to explore. Have either of you ever
thought why this country is such a treasurehouse of the old and
valuable?"

Thane and Dunbar exchanged a glance but stayed silent.
Mackenzie got to his feet and went over to his study window.
The view was out across wooded hills, with higher, snow-flecked
mountains in the distant background.

"As a nation, Britain spent generations fighting wars overseas
and building an empire," he said grimly. "In the process, wher-
ever they happened to be, our ancestors had the practical habit
of acquiring or looting anything they thought could be of value
and shipping it back home."

"Souvenirs?" suggested Thane.

"Their equivalent," said Lord Mackenzie. "Don't look too
closely at the origins of some of the Crown Jewels. Or how most
of Scotland's aristocracy got their original wealth." He shrugged.
"We weren't the only country doing that, and it's only part of
the picture. But what makes us unique is almost nine hundred
years without invasion—even in two World Wars. While Europe
was regularly gutting itself, we stayed relatively intact. Our antiques, acquired or native, remained undamaged, maturing in
value."

Thane nodded. "And now everyone wants them?"

"Everyone with money," corrected Mackenzie. "Americans,

Europeans, Arab oil sheiks—mostly as an investment." He grimaced. "That aspect had its attractions to me, apart from liking what I had." He paused and glanced significantly at Dunbar. "However, your sergeant didn't come here to be lectured."

Thane took the hint. "I'd like Sergeant Dunbar to talk with your housekeeper and her husband."

Lord Mackenzie nodded. Getting up and leaving them, Francey Dunbar seemed glad to escape.

"You reckoned there was more you could tell me," said Thane, as soon as the study door had closed.

"Yes." The little judge went over to a desk near the window, opened a drawer, and brought over a large booklet. He placed it open in front of Thane, pointing at a page which showed several colour photographs of crystal and porcelain vases. "On the left— the one with enamel work. That's Florentine crystal. It was stolen from a man named Lennox in Fife, one of the first people to be hit in these robberies."

Thane looked up at him. "You're sure?"

Mackenzie nodded. "This also happens to be the catalogue of a sale held last month in a New York auction room. I correspond with a friend over there. He sent it, I spotted the vase—but I haven't told Lennox." He paused and shrugged. "What good would it do? There's nothing more difficult than proving title to an antique. The auction firm is honest enough, and certainly sold it in good faith."

Thane frowned his surprise. "There's Interpol, the New York Police—"

"The best police in the world would get lost in a maze—who sold it, where it originated. You're in legal territory, Thane. *My* territory." Mackenzie shook his head. "Do I really help Lennox if I start him hiring packs of lawyers, send him plunging into international litigation in an attempt to get his property back? I don't think so." He tapped the catalogue. "But this at least proves where some of these antiques are going. Maybe my muskets and horse pistols will be in the next issue."

Picking up the catalogue, he returned it to the desk drawer.

Thane got to his feet and walked over to examine a small painting hanging on the opposite wall. It was a study of a ballerina, the style delicate, the colours cool and restrained.

"My Degas," said Mackenzie, coming up behind him. "My—ah —fake Degas. Interested?"

Thane nodded. "I like it."

"It's a beautiful forgery." The little judge ran a hand over his close-cropped grey hair, and gave a whimsical smile. "Only an expert could tell."

Thane nodded. "Is it insured as a Degas?"

"No. Her Majesty's judges are barred from deceit—certainly where it might involve gain."

"Your average crook wouldn't have left it." Thane touched the painting lightly with his fingertips, a thought firming in his mind, one he decided to keep to himself. "Suppose you're right in another direction, that this team have been staying comparatively low-key, just rehearsing for something big. Why play it that way?"

"To establish outlets, prove their capabilities to—well, foreign interests. It's a feeling, nothing more. A judge tends to see crime in terms of patterns, of progressions. I may be totally wrong. Or they may plan to clean out the damned National Gallery next week." He dismissed the problem with a grimace, went over to a cupboard and opened it. "You'll have a dram before you go? At least my whisky stayed intact—or I'd probably have lost a housekeeper into the bargain."

There was a choice of bottles, and Perthshire malts were famed. Thane settled for a rare, peaty-flavoured Glenturret, blinked at the size of measures the little judge poured, and knew it would have been a mortal sin to ask for water.

"To crime," said Lord Mackenzie, raising his glass. "It keeps us both in a job."

Thane grinned and sipped his drink. "Your Ransom Trust secretary offered me another job yesterday—security adviser for her Antiques Fair."

"Shona?" Mackenzie showed mild, amused surprise. "An enterprising young woman, like her brother. Peter Barry runs a business consultancy—how to make money despite trade unions and the Inland Revenue. Did she persuade you?"

"I'm getting her some help."

Mackenzie nodded his thanks.

They talked on for a few minutes, and another side of Bloody Mac's character showed itself. He was a shrewd connoisseur of whisky in general and the local Perthshire distilleries in particular. Then, finishing his drink, Thane made to leave.

The judge escorted him to the front door. The garden area was bathed in sunlight and Francey Dunbar was standing lazily beside their car.

"Thane." Mackenzie chuckled and laid a hand on his arm. "It looks like you can't escape. Here's someone you should meet."

A small car, dark green in colour, was coming up the driveway. It cleared the rhododendrons, slowed, and came to a halt a short distance from where they were standing. It was a Fiat. The driver was a girl with long, dark hair, and as Thane watched, the passenger door opened and Peter Barry got out. He waved a greeting, then opened one of the rear doors.

Francey Dunbar had stopped lounging. He looked towards Thane, his thin face showing a mixture of surprise and uncertainty, uncertainty that grew as Barry brought out a lightweight folding wheelchair, opened it out with practiced skill, and took it round to the driver's door. Lord Mackenzie stayed where he was, still smiling.

"Leave them," he said quietly. "Shona prefers it that way." He glanced at Thane. "Of course, you wouldn't know—Shona had polio as a child. That's why she's such a keen worker for the Trust, and her brother doesn't come far behind."

The driver's door opened. Without fuss or apparent effort, Shona Barry slid from behind the wheel and swung herself into the wheelchair. She said something to her brother, then propelled herself briskly across the gravel towards the house door.

"Paralysis of both legs," murmured Mackenzie. "Until then,

she was something of a schoolgirl athlete." He took a couple of steps forward, beaming. "You're first, as usual, Shona."

"It's the way she drives," complained Peter Barry, coming up behind her. He was carrying a briefcase and gave Thane a friendly nod. "Superintendent, this sister of mine drives like a maniac."

Shona Barry laughed. She was slim, with an attractive face and white, even teeth. She was wearing a dark-green trouser suit with a black shirt, open at the neck to show a thin gold chain. Brushing back her long hair with one hand, she gave a mock grimace of penitence.

"Just now and again," she protested. "Hello, Superintendent. Peter spotted you as we came in."

"And warned you," said Barry dryly. He turned to Lord Mackenzie. "If we're too early—"

"No, we've finished our business," said Mackenzie. He laid a hand on Shona Barry's shoulder. "What's this about trying to recruit the police into our ranks?"

"I've arranged some help," volunteered Thane. "You should hear from one of the Crime Prevention teams fairly quickly."

"I'll let you know if we don't," she warned good-naturedly, then frowned. "The way things are, with so many robberies, I think it makes sense. There's going to be a lot of valuable property in this Antiques Fair."

"If it works out," qualified Peter Barry.

"It should," said Mackenzie.

"What's involved?" Thane asked her.

"A lot," she said. Strong fingers touched the rims of her chair and edged it around to face him directly. "It'll be a touring show —the idea's not totally new. A collection of loaned antiques on view, experts present who'll value anything old that people care to bring along, lectures, a film show—"

Thane nodded. "When?"

"Next month, all going well, starting in Ayrshire," said Peter Barry. "But there's a lot to be done. If promises come through, it'll be a road show carrying some real surprises." He saw

Thane's reaction and grinned. "We won't take any risks, Superintendent."

"We daren't," murmured Lord Mackenzie. "Not when we've got the damned stuff on loan."

"Good luck with it," said Thane. "If you get to Glasgow I might come along." He glanced at his watch, then across to where Francey Dunbar was now behind the wheel of their Ford, and turned to Lord Mackenzie. "I'll be in touch."

The judge nodded.

Thane said goodbye, left them, and went over to the car. As he got in, Peter Barry was helping his sister manoeuvre the wheelchair up the few steps to the porch of Drum Lodge.

"You never think about it," said Francey Dunbar, starting the engine. "I mean—well, you walk around, someone else can't." He shook his head. "Though, when I saw her at first, in that car—"

"Yes." Thane had been equally startled, the description of the woman who had picked up Anna Marshton flashing through his mind. He sighed, watching the group on the porch disappear into the house. "I'll tell you about her. Let's move."

Dunbar set the car rolling. As they reached the end of the driveway, two more cars were turning in. The Ransom Trust committee was gathering.

It was an hour's drive to Edinburgh, heading southeast, coming in as part of the heavy traffic using the high, steel-supported ribbon of the Forth Road Bridge, the blue waters of the River Forth flecked with shipping far below and the North Sea a greying expanse spreading out to the horizon.

Francey Dunbar knew the capital city well enough to quit the main traffic flow. He used a collection of side roads to bring the car into the heart of the capital, the bustle of Princes Street, with the commanding bulk of Edinburgh Castle looking down on everything from its picture-postcard setting.

Traffic on Princes Street was moving at a snail's pace. But they soon turned off again and Dunbar stopped the car in a side street. The only space was under a NO PARKING sign, but it was just a stone's throw from the wine bar. As they got out, the traditional One O'Clock Gun boomed its time signal from the castle.

"One day they'll make a mistake," said Dunbar solemnly, while the air still shivered with the echoing bang. "They'll have a live round up the spout. It's going to make a hole in some hellish expensive property."

"Then they'll blame Glasgow," agreed Thane, admiring the way the impressive Georgian buildings almost sparkled in the sunlight. He sniffed the decidedly different East Coast tang in the air and felt hungry. "All right, lead the way."

The wine bar was busy. It had oak panelling to ceiling height, screened booths, an Italian staff, and a menu chalked on a blackboard behind the bar counter. Sandra Craig and a dark-haired, stockily built man were in a booth halfway along. She was sipping a glass of wine, and her companion nursed a mug of beer.

"We've eaten. I didn't know how long you'd be," she said apologetically as Thane and Dunbar took seats on the other side of the table. She indicated her companion. "Sergeant Brownlea, Edinburgh C.I.D."

"Dave Brownlea, sir." The dark-haired man shook hands as the introductions were completed, then thumbed towards Sandra. "I've been kidnapped. A mate of mine in your Edinburgh mob sent her round, and I'm not sure about after that."

Francey Dunbar grunted. "With her, it's either charm or a wristlock." He looked at the menu. "What have you left that's worth eating?"

"Try the tortellini," suggested Sandra, eyeing him frostily. "But it's probably too good for your peasant palate." She leaned towards Thane in a way that strained her sweater and made the Edinburgh sergeant's eyes widen in appreciation. "Dave handled the Dutchman case, sir—and he knows the local antiques world."

Sergeant Brownlea nodded. "That's why Hans Schilton came my way. We had him marked as one of the Flying Dutchmen team, and anything in the city that involves the antiques scene is punted my way. If I can help—"

"We need any shortcuts you can give us," said Thane gratefully. He paused as a waiter came over, ordered a risotto while Dunbar chose the tortellini, added a carafe of wine and another beer for Brownlea, then turned to the Edinburgh man again. "What's the story with Schilton?"

"Well, he claimed he was mugged," said Brownlea. "A taxi driver found him about one A.M. and took him to hospital, and the casualty department reported it." He paused, took a gulp of beer, and shook his head. "Through here, if you're mugged they don't leave your wallet in your pocket and a gold watch on your wrist. Schilton was worked over, sir—but don't ask me why."

Thane glanced at Sandra, and she gave the faintest of nods.

"How about guessing aloud, Sergeant?" he suggested.

Brownlea winced. "I can't back it with fact."

Francey Dunbar grinned. "Dave, we thrive on that kind of story."

"So try us," invited Thane. The wine had arrived and he let Francey take charge of the carafe, pushing Brownlea's fresh beer across to him.

"He was done up," said Brownlea. "Warned off."

"Because the Dutch team were trying to get their fingers in someone else's pie?"

Brownlea blinked. "Yes, but—"

"What about where he was found?"

"A lane off the Royal Mile. Not far from a junk shop run by a female called Auntie Rose—we've had her twice for handling stolen antiques, but never made it stick. I tried her, but—" He left it at that and shrugged.

Thane nodded. "How about now? Are the Dutch team back yet?"

"No sign of them," said Brownlea. "Maybe somebody did us a favour. In fact, as far as Edinburgh's concerned, things are quiet."

"No strangers on the antiques scene?"

Brownlea grinned and glanced at Sandra. "She asked me that. There's an American dealer in town, buying like mad—he's been around for a couple of weeks. We checked him out, as soon as he started advertising he was in the market—that's standard drill."

"He's legitimate," said Sandra. "With his kind of bank references he has to be." She sighed. "Edward Sarraut of Los Angeles, six feet tall, suntanned, wants to take me for a steak dinner—"

"You've seen him?" asked Francey Dunbar, surprised.

"About an hour ago," she said. "In his hotel—I told him I could offer him something interesting."

Dunbar spluttered. "Like what?"

"Wash out your mind," she said sweetly. "I've an old jade necklace that belonged to my grandmother. He said that wasn't quite his line, but the steak dinner offer stands."

The two ordered meals arrived, and the conversation dried while Thane and Dunbar ate. The food was good, but Thane was still only halfway through his risotto when the waiter returned and murmured to Brownlea. Brownlea leaned across the table.

"Phone call for you from Glasgow," he told Thane. "Someone named Felix—says he knew you'd be here."

Sighing, Thane abandoned his meal and followed the waiter through the wine bar to a telephone booth in a corner. He closed the door, lifted the receiver, and spoke to Joe Felix.

"It's the postmortem report on Anna Marshton," explained Felix over the line. "Inspector Moss said you'd want to know."

"Go on." Thane smiled to himself, cradling the receiver against his shoulder. Phil Moss was one ally he could count on.

"Time of death stays as before, between midnight and two A.M. She was strangled all right, but she'd taken a blow on the head first—enough to knock her out. There's not much else, except she'd had a few drinks some hours earlier and hadn't eaten much." Felix paused, the line good enough to convey the sound of paper rustling. "On the laboratory side, he says they've next to nothing so far. The Marshton woman's flat was a dead loss, except that it looks as though someone went around wiping fingerprint surfaces. They've only a few which were Anna Marshton's, and the rest are—uh—yours or Sandra's."

"That would make them happy," said Thane sarcastically. He pursed his lips. "Anything fresh your side?"

"No. Except that same character who phoned this morning called again. He still won't say what it's about," reported Felix.

"How about Malky Darvel?" persisted Thane.

"Your coffin-maker? Sorry—no word from him."

"Right." Thane's eyes strayed to the blank wall of the booth. Amid a varied scribble of telephone numbers some sad soul had written "Even when I try to think young, I can't get under fifty." He grinned, then said, "Joe, there's an oddity about the break-in at Bloody Mac's place. You've got the file. Who carried the insurance risk?"

"Hold on, boss." Felix was absent for a moment, then came back on the line. "You're in the right place. He's covered by Clanmore Mutual in Edinburgh. Their head office is in George Street. But—uh—" His curiosity was plain.

"We'll handle it." Without further explanation, Thane said goodbye and hung up.

Leaving the telephone booth, he went back through the crowded restaurant area and rejoined the others. His half-eaten risotto was still on the table, and now it lay cold and unappetising. Shoving it aside, he decided to stay hungry.

"That was a progress report from Joe," he said dryly. "There isn't any." It was near enough the truth, and he left it at that. "Dave—"

"Sir?" The Edinburgh sergeant met his gaze.

"I want to meet this 'Auntie Rose' at her junk shop. But it would be better if you stayed outside—understood?"

Dave Brownlea looked perturbed, but nodded.

"And us?" asked Francey Dunbar.

"You'll be earning your keep." He gave his sergeant a half-smile. "Sandra comes with me, you can use her car. For a start, check out an insurance angle. The Clanmore Mutual office is in George Street. Get to someone at the top of their tree. Find out how many of their people could get hold of an insurance policy's details."

Dunbar sucked his teeth, putting two and two together. "Drum Lodge?"

Thane nodded.

There was a parking ticket waiting on the Ford when they left the wine bar. Three pairs of eyes turned to Brownlea, who flushed, removed the ticket, and tucked it into his pocket.

"Where afterwards?" asked Dunbar.

"Our own place," Thane told him. The Crime Squad office in Edinburgh was modest in size, had its own workload, but made a good base. "But radio if you've any problems."

Dunbar nodded and walked away.

Brownlea in the rear seat, Thane driving with Sandra Craig beside him, the Ford started off.

The route was along the congested length of Princes Street, an obstacle course of traffic lights and swarms of shoppers. Brownlea navigating, the car took a right turn at the Post Office corner, headed across North Bridge, then took a left into the historic Royal Mile, the ancient heart of the capital's tourist territory.

Tall, centuries-old buildings of grey stone, close-paned windows and abruptly pitched roofs lay on either side of the narrow street. Cars with registration plates from a dozen countries clogged its length, tourists of every race, age and nationality seemed to be inspecting the windows of its tiny old-fashioned shops. The Royal Mile was history in stone, a legend for each narrow lane and tiny courtyard.

"Makes a change for you, I suppose," suggested Brownlea mildly, leaning forward. "I mean, Glasgow isn't exactly on the package-tour map."

"We try to keep it that way," said Thane. He winked at Brownlea through the driving mirror. "All right, you're the mysterious East. Now tell me more about Auntie Rose."

"She's not so old—late forties, maybe." Brownlea pondered his words. "Dyed blonde, English—came up from London with her first husband, who was a safeblower. He died, she remarried and became Rose Cadden, kicked the new husband out after six months and opened the shop—that was years ago."

"Sounds interesting," said Sandra cheerfully.

"If you like them hard as nails," said Brownlea. "The way she works, she handles only a few thieves—genuine pros, mostly the antique jewellery end. Not the heavier stuff." He nodded ahead. "Turn left here, then stop."

They pulled into a lane almost under the shadow of the old Canongate Tolbooth, parked the car, and Brownlea pointed ahead to a small shop with bright-pink woodwork.

"That's it. You're sure you don't want me along?"

"No," said Thane, "I don't."

They left him and walked along the granite cobblestones of the lane. Close up, the shop with the pink paintwork was even smaller than they'd thought. The sign above the door said quite simply AUNTIE ROSE, and the window gave a view of a collection of everything from old fire irons and brassware to a case of war medals and a battered rocking horse.

A bell clanged as they opened the door and went in. There was no counter, and the floor space was a maze of stacked paintings, black varnished furniture, and the dull glint of copper pans. At the back, a stuffed bear guarded a curtained doorway. As the door closed behind them, the curtain jerked open and a woman stepped out.

"Yes?" She gave them a disinterested, totally professional smile. "Looking for something, are you?"

Thane drew a deep breath. Brownlea's description was reasonably accurate. But he hadn't mentioned that Auntie Rose was built on Amazon lines, and a few other details. The dyed-blond hair went with a rawboned face, heavy lipstick, and a dark-green dress cut tight to emphasise an ample bust.

"Just you, I think," he said flatly. "Police." He showed his warrant card as he spoke. "A few minutes of your time, Rose."

She swore, shoved past them, and locked the shop door with a grim resignation.

"Well?" She looked Sandra up and down, then Thane. "You're new, both of you."

"Crime Squad," said Thane. "On a day trip from Glasgow."

"The heavies." She grinned, unperturbed. "So?"

"Hans Schilton," said Thane. "Who beat him up and why?"

She shrugged. "How the hell should I know?"

"Pillow talk," suggested Sandra calmly. "He left here around midnight, didn't he?" She smiled at the woman's glare. "You don't look totally past it."

"Thanks," said the woman sarcastically. She tapped her fingers angrily against the lid of a copper pot. "You're wasting my time. I can't tell you anything."

"That's what you told Sergeant Brownlea," said Thane. He leaned against an ugly Victorian chest and sighed. "We're different, Rose. We can play dirty."

"Meaning?" She faced him belligerently.

"Little things," he said vaguely. "Like spread the word in a few places that you're a Crime Squad target. Plant a man with big boots and a camera outside your door, taking anyone's picture who comes or goes."

"Turn the place over a few times," suggested Sandra, matching his mood. "We're good at that."

"But it's hell for business," said Thane. "We could wipe you out as a fence, Rose. Like that." He snapped his fingers. "Not that you're worth the effort. But Hans Schilton is. So which is it?"

The woman swore, grabbed the copper pot by the handle, and swung it at him. He ducked and the pot brushed his shoulder, then clanged hard against the Victorian woodwork he'd been leaning on.

The pot swung back for another try. But Sandra Craig was there first. A yelp of pain came from Auntie Rose as the redhead caught her in a wristlock which forced an arm hard up behind her back. Dropping the pot, the older woman tried to struggle free, gave another involuntary yelp as the grip tightened, then gave up.

"Call her off," she surrendered. "Hans was here."

Thane nodded and Sandra released her. Straightening, rubbing her arm, the woman tossed back her hair and grimaced at them.

"All right, I'm not looking for extra problems," she said wearily. "What do you want to know?"

"Why it happened, how it happened," suggested Sandra.

Auntie Rose glared at her. "I'm talking to the organ grinder, not his bitch monkey," she said, then faced Thane. "Just understand I'm not involved. Hans came here a lot, but I didn't handle any stuff for his outfit. Right?"

"Purely social," agreed Thane.

"That last trip, according to Hans, they came to Scotland for two reasons. One was—well, their usual. Fair enough?"

"A Flying Dutchmen raid," said Thane. "The other?"

"They market their stuff through half a dozen European antique dealers. Real operators, the kind you'll never get near. One of those dealers, a Frenchman, told them he'd been buying from someone new, someone here in Edinburgh. Small shipments but good quality and—"

"And the promise of something big to come?" suggested Thane.

"Yes." She stared at him in surprise. "You mean—"

"Just tell it," Thane said.

The woman shrugged. "This new boy wanted to set up a deal. It was going to be big all right—big enough to have the Frenchman worried, though the new boy seemed to have an inside track, knew what he was doing." She paused, still aggressive even in defeat. "Anyway, the French operator suggested Hans and his friends should take over, use the new boy as junior partner."

"But—" Sandra stopped it there as Thane gave her a quick headshake.

He asked, "They made contact?"

"They did." The woman nodded. "Hans got the job, made the contact, and was told to go to hell. He doesn't take no for an

answer—I know that. So he tried again. He came here afterwards, and—"

"And got beaten up when he left?"

"You've got it." The rawboned face tightened. "I saw him
again, once, before he was shipped back to Holland. There were
two of them, clubs and big boots style. When they were finished,
they told him to stay off their patch—that next time they'd either
cripple him or kill him."

"Nice people," said Thane. He rubbed a hand along his chin.
"Who's running them, Rose?"

"He didn't tell me," she said. "With Hans, if he doesn't tell
you, you don't ask."

Thane looked at her for a moment, decided she meant it, and
nodded. "Think he'll be back?"

"One of these days." Her lips shaped a fractional smile. "Yes,
I think so. But his team don't go in for heavy muscle. The new
boy can sink or swim on his own."

"In your shoes, I'd hope he drowned," said Sandra.

"Men," she sighed. "They foul things up for everyone."

Sandra nodded. "What about this local team? Do you know
anything about them?"

"No. Just that his contact was here, in Edinburgh." She turned
to Thane. "But I'll tell you one thing, for free. This antiques job,
whatever it is, is soon. Hans said before the end of this month.
And you know something? I'd almost like you to nail the swine."

Thane and Sandra Craig exchanged a startled glance. The
month would be ended in a few days. Yet Thane guessed the big
dyed-blond woman was telling the truth, telling them all she
knew.

"Let's start again," he suggested slowly. "From the top—and
I'm not collecting your Dutch pals. I want the new boy, Rose."

They went through her story twice. She didn't vary it, couldn't
expand on it.

"That's it, then," said Thane at last. "Thanks."

She gave him a shrug, saying nothing. Nodding to Sandra, he
headed for the door, opened it, then looked back.

"Tell me something different, Rose," he said mildly. "You're in the trade. How's the market for old brass candlesticks?"

"Candlesticks?" She blinked.

"I've a pair at home," he explained. "Any idea what they could be worth?"

Auntie Rose drew a deep breath. She was still explaining in precise, clinical detail what Thane could do with the candlesticks as they got out and closed the shop door.

Dave Brownlea had moved into the Ford's front passenger seat when they reached the end of the lane. He gestured at the radio as they got in.

"There was a message for you," he told Thane. "I acknowledged. Sergeant Dunbar says could you join him at the Claymore Mutual office."

"Right." Thane got behind the wheel, started the car, but let it idle for a moment while he thought. "Sandra, I'm going to drop you off in Princes Street. See your pet American dealer again—for real this time. Ask about market whispers, any hint of the unusual coming up for auction—anything else that might point us towards a target."

"And bang goes my dinner date," she said ruefully.

He started the car, eased it back out into the street, set it moving along the Royal Mile again, then swore suddenly, braked, and stopped with the wheels rubbing the kerb.

A familiar, bald-headed figure was ambling along the pavement towards them. Getting out, Thane intercepted Malky Darvel as he was about to walk past.

"You." The plump-faced coffin-maker was startled and not totally pleased. "Hey, look, this won't do my reputation any good—"

"I'll say sorry another time," Thane told him. "Where are you heading? To Auntie Rose?"

"Her?" Darvel paled visibly at the notion. "No way. She scares me. Why?"

"She's not in a mood for visitors." Thane paused as a chattering group of tourists went past. "I'm not crowding your pitch, Malky. We had to come through. Any luck so far?"

"Picture-frame glass like I'm after is hard to find," said Darvel. Then he winked. "I'm on my way to see—well, someone else in the trade, right?" He gestured ahead, vaguely. "You don't really want to know where, Mr. Thane."

There were at least four antique shops within a stone's throw, Thane had no idea how many more within a couple of minutes' walk.

"Your business," he agreed. "But—?"

"I've heard a thing or two," admitted the little coffin-maker. "Let me put it together, eh?" He glanced around cautiously. "Tell you one thing. Some hard men have been brought through from Glasgow—real imports. The kind that cost more than beer money."

"Any names?"

"Give me time, eh?" Darvel refused to be hurried. "Edinburgh brain, Glasgow muscle—there's a book like that, isn't there, Mr. Thane?" He frowned. "Never read it, mind you. But it's called *A Tale of Two Cities*—something like that, anyway."

"I don't think the story is the same, Malky," said Thane.

"Didn't get it right then, did he?" Darvel's face split in a grin. "Look, I'll see you later, before I go back to Glasgow. Fair enough?"

"Where?"

The man thought quickly. "The Castle. Nice an' public, yet nobody around but day-trippers an' soldiers. Make it about six o'clock, near where they've got those old guns."

"The Half-Moon Battery." Thane nodded.

"On your own," suggested Darvel. "It's safer that way."

He walked off.

CHAPTER 5

For some reason known only to God, the City Fathers of Edinburgh and perhaps the Scottish Tourist Board—though not necessarily in that order—there was a kilted pipe band parading along Princes Street. The result was a major traffic snarl-up, the pipers looked hot and sticky under their feather bonnets, and the drummers rattled out their part of the action with a mechanical lack of enthusiasm. But they were followed by a minor horde of delighted tourists, and it was the kind of thing that sold a lot of camera film.

Caught in the traffic, it took Thane twice as long as he'd expected to get to the Clanmore Mutual office in George Street. He'd dropped off Sandra Craig and Dave Brownlea along the way, the Edinburgh sergeant with work of his own to do. Brownlea had stoically refrained from asking what had happened at their meeting with Auntie Rose, and, beyond telling him that it had been helpful, Thane had left it that way.

But the word "helpful" was an understatement. Slotting the Ford into a vacated parking space, Colin Thane sighed to himself as he got out, locked the car, and fed change into the parking meter.

He was under no illusion about why the woman had talked, and it had little to do with the way they'd leaned on her. That had merely allowed her to overcome her normal antipathy towards anything carrying a warrant card and leave the way clear for what she really wanted, a chance for revenge.

So the antiques gang was based on the capital, and Bloody Mac's educated guess had been right—the "big job" was still to come, and that very soon if Auntie Rose had it right. Colin Thane looked across the street at the tall, elegant building which housed the Clanmore Mutual headquarters with a sense of gloomy foreboding, a sense that things could only get worse.

When it came to projecting an image, Clanmore Mutual believed in offering visiting policyholders a blend of cool comfort and brisk efficiency. Their public counter area had wall-to-wall carpeting, deep armchairs in the event of anyone having to be kept waiting, enough greenery to stock a small garden, and a series of carefully hung seascape prints. The counter was covered in black padded vinyl, and the girls behind it, the obvious front rank of a filtering process, appeared to have been picked to match a uniformly high standard of looks and, whatever their intelligence, an ability to smile.

Thane was expected. One of the counter girls emerged, took him over to an elevator concealed behind a screen of potted palms, and they rode up to the fifth floor.

The atmosphere was different there, totally workmanlike, as if Clanmore's directors felt the front-office expenditure had to be balanced somehow to satisfy their canny Scottish consciences. Thane followed the girl along a corridor where the walls were a stark cream and the flooring a dull, scuffed lino. She stopped at the last of several doors, knocked, then opened it and gestured him in.

As the door closed behind him, Thane glanced around a large, plainly furnished office. It had a window which overlooked George Street and gave a panoramic view of Edinburgh's rooftops. Standing beside it, Francey Dunbar gave him a nod as the other man in the room came over, offering an outstretched hand.

"Superintendent." The handshake was the "firm sincere clasp" variety, but moist. "I'm John Talbot, chief claims executive. Your sergeant has been telling me about your—ah—slight problem."

"Good," Thane said. The insurance executive was a tall, plump man in a dark business suit, white shirt and carefully knotted company tie. Behind the welcome there was a faint hint of worry or perhaps annoyance. "Any help you can give stays informal—for now, anyway."

"I hope so." Talbot frowned. "But what your sergeant suggests couldn't happen. There's no way confidential client information could be leaked from here."

"Francey?" Thane raised an eyebrow in Dunbar's direction.

"All their records are computerised," said Dunbar. "Everything on tape, punch-up display units for everyone but the office cat." He shrugged. "I don't trust computers, that's all."

"And I've explained, there are total safeguards in the system," said John Talbot, reddening. "I chaired the blasted committee that decided on them—damn it, I'll show you."

He led Thane over to his desk, Francey Dunbar ambling at their heels. There was a VDU screen and keyboard built into the desk unit, and Talbot planked himself down on his chair, facing it.

"Right." He eyed them with confidence. "I'll skip the basics—that a computer is a worktool, nothing more. Most of our employees have legitimate access to a VDU terminal, like this one. They use them to recall policy information, assemble new policy business for printout, store claims records, premium payments—routine office work."

"Routine," agreed Thane. Uninvited, he drew a chair over and sat beside Talbot.

"Your sergeant is interested in Lord Mackenzie's domestic insurance," said Talbot. "He had the policy number—"

"And a couple of others," murmured Dunbar. He glanced at Thane. "I checked with Joe Felix. Three Clanmore clients are on the robberies list."

"He had the policy number," repeated Talbot, undeterred. "It wasn't necessary." His stubby fingers tapped the terminal keyboard and the screen showed a row of figures. "If we have name and address, we can locate the policy details—policy number first." He tapped two keys as he spoke. The row of figures vanished and the screen quivered, then was filled with print.

"There we have it—Lord Mackenzie's insurance cover, but only in basic detail."

Thane frowned at the screen. Some of the information was in plain language, from annual premium through to total insured value. But beneath that were three groups of coded figures.

"You want more than that?" asked Talbot, pleased with himself. "You can't. Unless, that is, the employee concerned has been authorised to use stage-one security coding. Like this." He tapped more keys and the screen changed.

This time, they were looking at a close-printed inventory list. Bloody Mac's collection of old weapons, his antique furniture and his silver were all there, each with a declared value. Thane checked it through carefully. There was no Degas painting listed.

"How many know that coding?" demanded Dunbar.

"Senior departmental staff," said Talbot. "No others." He pointed to a numbered code at the bottom of the display. "And even they can't acquire this stage—security details. That requires another coded request, and that can be made only by a claims surveyor or above."

"Show me," suggested Thane.

"I can't," said Talbot triumphantly. "Not 'won't'—'can't.' We keep access to a minimum. If I need to know, then I call in someone who has access." He beamed at them. "Well?"

Francey Dunbar scowled. "All right, tell us about them," he said. "How much could you have on record?"

"Anything that might affect the risk—or the premium," said Talbot, sitting back. "Sometimes we insist on certain security systems being installed. Last week, for instance, I advised a diamond merchant who operates from home that he'd have to comply with several things we required before his cover was renewed." He chuckled. "It doesn't always work that way, of course. Sometimes it's safer to offer only partial cover, negate the 'moral hazard' syndrome."

Thane looked at him blankly.

"An economic theory, Superintendent," said Talbot indulgently. "One that makes sound sense at several commercial levels. The average individual only properly values something he possesses if it has cost him money or genuine effort." He glanced slyly at Dunbar. "Your sergeant might translate that as easy come, easy go. In the insurance world, our translation is that certain individuals take a lot less care of their property if it happens to be fully insured."

"So you keep a grip on them where it hurts," suggested Dunbar.

Talbot shrugged. "Insurance is a risk business, but still a business. We're careful."

Dunbar grunted. "Or hard-faced."

"No, that's our shareholders," said Talbot. "But we don't take chances—and that applies to our records."

"But at least a few of your people, the ones with access to the security code, could tap the computer for information about alarm systems," persisted Thane. "And a larger number could pull out information about high-value items insured."

"Yes," agreed Talbot.

"I'd like a list of names with security-code access."

For a long moment Talbot sat tight-lipped. Then he nodded.

"That's on the computer too, Superintendent. Part of staff records—blocked, except to management. I can give you it here."

"I'll leave Sergeant Dunbar to get it." Thane got to his feet. "We'll also need names of maintenance personnel, technicians, anyone else who might be involved."

"Whatever you want," said Talbot. He was still puzzled. "Why *this* company, Superintendent?"

"Somebody has to come top of the list," Thane told him. "But you won't be alone."

The Scottish Crime Squad in Edinburgh followed a fairly similar pattern to its parent in the west. It had a token presence in the regional Lothian and Borders headquarters, but its real base was an inconspicuous building in a side street near to Leith Docks.

Colin Thane got there about 4 P.M. and was met by the shift officer, a lanky detective inspector named Malcolm who greeted him with a friendly curiosity.

"It's the usual story, sir," admitted Malcolm. "My boys like to feel they can handle their own patch. So when we knew your team had moved through—"

"They got temperamental?" Thane grimaced at him. "Tell them this got dumped in my lap. It's Edinburgh today, God knows where tomorrow."

"I'm not complaining," said Malcolm cheerfully. "We're short-handed anyway. For my money, you're welcome to it."

The only spare room available was a small cubicle of an office with a table, chair and telephone and not much more. An orderly brought Thane a mug of coffee and two telex messages which had been waiting his arrival, then he was left alone.

Lighting a cigarette, sipping the coffee, Thane read the telex messages through.

One was from Joe Felix, a simple confirmation of the insurance policy numbers he'd already given to Francey Dunbar. The other, more surprisingly, was from Maggie Fyffe and consisted of two words.

CALL ME.

Frowning, he lifted the telephone and dialled the direct line. In another moment, he was speaking to her.

"Trouble?" he asked.

"No," she said. "Just trying to keep the wheels turning. Joe Felix told you about this man who keeps phoning?"

"Yes, but—" Thane frowned at the receiver.

"I took the call last time." She paused. "No name, and wouldn't tell me what it's about. Still, I've set up a meeting for you."

"Look, Maggie—" he tried again.

"I've set it up," she said firmly. "Tomorrow morning, seven A.M., outside Shields Road underground station. Don't blame me —it's *his* choice, time and place."

"What do I do, wear a red rose?" asked Thane.

"He says he'll know you," Maggie Fyffe countered. "And this should interest you. Joe Felix had set up an intercept, expecting he'd try again. The call came from a street telephone box near Harald Street."

That made a difference, a considerable difference. Thane thanked her, checked there was nothing else happening he should know about, and hung up.

He drank the rest of his coffee and smoked the cigarette through, thinking over the way things stood. If there was a gap in what he'd done so far, it wasn't obvious. As for the way the situation was shaping—he stubbed his cigarette grimly in the tin lid which passed as an ashtray.

He'd been in the same kind of situation in cases before. The stage Phil Moss had once described as looking for a needle in a haystack blindfold, wearing boxing gloves. But a good half of police work was like that, keeping going, eliminating, discarding, then being ready to move fast when a situation became positive.

And perhaps, if Malky Darvel came through—he glanced at his watch. It was still close on two hours before he was due to meet the little coffin-maker.

After that, the evening might lead anywhere. The thought prompted another and, lifting the telephone again, he dialled his home number.

It rang for several seconds before Mary answered. When she did, her voice sounded unusually tight and strained.

"How's Edinburgh?" she asked.

"Still standing. I'm pretty much the same," he said. "But I could be late home."

"Which is it?" she asked resignedly. "'Don't keep a meal for me' or 'Don't wait up for me'?"

"I don't know," he admitted. "Not yet."

"I wish—" She stopped it there.

"Something wrong?" he asked, sensing there was.

"Tommy again," she said. "I could use some help with him, Colin. I—" He heard their doorbell sound in the background, and she broke off for a moment, then came back on the line. "It's a woman from down the street. I'd better go and see what she wants. But we'll need to talk about Tommy."

"We will," he promised. "I'll get back as soon as I can."

He hung up with a sigh, swore, lit another cigarette without thinking, then scowled at it. He had listened to plenty of other cops talk about problems they'd had with their children but never paid too much attention. Now it looked as if it was his turn.

But there wasn't much he could do, not until he was home and found out what had been happening.

Detective Inspector Malcolm looked in a little later and stayed for about ten minutes. The Edinburgh man was in a chatty mood, obviously keen to collect any headquarters gossip, and Thane finally got rid of him by the excuse of going through to the communications room to see if any fresh telex messages had come in.

He was on his way back from there, crossing the main office area, when Sandra Craig walked in. Just behind her came a young, heavily built man with fair hair, a matching beard, and a tanned complexion. Looking around with interest, he followed her over as she came straight towards Thane.

"I brought a visitor," said Sandra. She glanced at the stranger. "You wanted to meet my boss. Here he is."

"Edward Sarraut," said the stranger cheerfully, holding out his hand. "Throw me out if you're busy, Superintendent, but this lady says you've been checking whether I'm genuine."

"You and some other people, Mr. Sarraut." Thane shook hands with the American dealer, who was casually dressed in dark slacks, a light-coloured sports jacket, and an open-necked shirt. "Does it worry you?"

"No." Sarraut chuckled. "Just makes me curious." He glanced at Sandra, an appreciative twinkle in his eyes. "She had me fooled first time, believe me. Then when she turned up again and showed that warrant card, I said I'd like to meet whoever was running the show."

"For 'like' read 'insisted,'" said Sandra Craig wryly, but with a matching twinkle in her eyes.

"That's right." Sarraut nodded seriously. "Look, Superintendent, I've got the general picture. You're chasing a gang of antiques thieves, their loot is being shipped abroad, so anyone like me has to be checked out." He paused. "I know what you're up against. That's why I'm here."

Thane glanced at Sandra and raised an eyebrow. She gave a slight nod, he beckoned them to follow him through to his temporary office.

"Sit down," he invited Sarraut, and perched himself on the table. "All right, tell me."

Sarraut pursed his lips. "Superintendent, back home I run a string of small galleries on the West Coast. To feed them, I'm over in Europe maybe half a dozen times a year. There are plenty others like me, playing a straight enough game." He gave a helpless shrug. "Hell, the odds are I've probably bought and sold stolen goods a few times without knowing it. That's inevitable in this business. But I don't want the underworld moving in any more than they have already—none of us do."

"If it happens, you're the loser," said Thane.

"Right." Sarraut grinned disarmingly. "It's self-protection, Superintendent. Otherwise, someday my personal world could hit the fan. The trouble is that an antique is just that—something old, usually with a pretty vague history. You've no idea most of the time whether there's another one like it or another few hundred."

"But you price on the first hope?" asked Thane. He leaned closer. "What's this trip been like?"

"So far, just normal," said Sarraut. "I've made plenty of private buys, gone bidding at a few auctions—the usual pattern. Nothing spectacular." He pointed towards Sandra, who was leaning against a wall. "The lady saw my purchase lists."

"There's nothing we're looking for on them," she agreed, breaking her silence. She glanced sideways at Sarraut. "Or that's how they read."

"Thanks," said Sarraut caustically. He scratched his beard for a moment, then turned to Thane again. "This other notion of yours, Superintendent—that there's something really big around this gang might go for." He shook his head. "That's a pretty wide field. But there's certainly nothing major in auction or exhibition terms until well after the end of the month."

"But—" prompted Sandra.

Sarraut grinned. "Persistent, isn't she? All right, stretch your time factor and there's one pretty crazy possibility." He glanced at his watch. "In fact, I'm due back at my hotel almost now to meet with some people about it. It's a touring antiques fair, for charity—"

"The Ransom Trust?" asked Thane sharply.

"Yes." Sarraut showed surprise. "Well, if you know about it—"

"Only a little."

"They've got big plans," said Sarraut. "That Barry girl and her brother don't take no for an answer. They've put the bite on some pretty amazing people, getting a loan of some damned valuable stuff. It's going to be like Aladdin's Cave on wheels."

Thane felt as if the little room had suddenly grown smaller.

"What do they want from you?" he demanded.

"My body, more or less," said Sarraut with a grimace. "Visiting American expert tells all—I'm checking if it's tax deductible." He glanced at his watch again and got to his feet. "I've got to go. My hotel is at the far end of Princes Street."

"I'm heading that way," Thane told him. "I'll give you a lift."

"I—uh—" Sarraut glanced towards Sandra Craig. "Well, I had that sort of organised."

"Detective Constable Craig has work to do," said Thane, and saw the redhead blink. Then she caught on, and gave a murmur of agreement.

"How about later?" asked Sarraut hopefully. "Like I said, there's this restaurant I know—"

"Make it for eight o'clock," Sandra told him. Then, cautiously, she added a warning. "I eat a lot."

"And she means it," said Thane.

He got Sarraut out before one irate detective constable could reply.

Edward Sarraut was living in the Ravenwood Hotel, modest in size but expensive. It was located in a quiet square near the Lothian Road end of Princes Street, the kind of place where there were trees, terraced Georgian houses, and a more than reasonable quota of Rolls-Royce cars in the parking bays.

Feeling the Crime Squad car rated like a poor relation, Thane eased it into a gap between a Camargue and a low-slung Ferrari, then followed Sarraut out.

"Mind if I come in for a moment?" he asked.

"Be my guest," said Sarraut cheerfully. He gestured towards a dark-green Fiat parked outside the Ravenwood's entrance. "Looks like they're here already."

They went in. Sarraut spoke briefly to the hall porter, then beckoned Thane towards the cocktail bar. Grinning, he led the way across to where Shona Barry had her wheelchair beside a table.

"I brought someone you know," he said, indicating Thane, then looked around, slightly puzzled. "Where's that brother of yours?"

"He'll be along. He had a business call to make." She smiled up at Thane. "You're really mixing in the antiques world, Superintendent. Maybe we'll trap you yet."

"It won't be easy." Thane took a chair, shook his head at Sarraut's offer of a drink, and considered Shona Barry for a moment while the American went off to order for her and himself. The dark-haired girl had all the looks and personality any woman could want. The wheelchair's significance shrank in one respect, became more bitter in another.

"Don't let it worry you," she said suddenly, as if reading his mind. "Look, I'm still one of the lucky ones—and I mean that." She paused. "Do I have to go on calling you 'Superintendent'?"

"Colin Thane." He drew a deep breath. "You put a lot into this Ransom Trust, don't you?"

She nodded. "I call it fighting back."

"And your brother?"

"The same. If that doesn't make us sound like a pair of fa-natics." Her eyes became serious. "Like to guess how many hos-pital research projects the Trust is funding?"

"I couldn't," he admitted.

"Fifteen. Forget Britain's Welfare State. Without us, most of those projects would fold up. But if even one makes some kind of a breakthrough, gives some kids the chance to get back on their feet again—" She stopped short and wrinkled her nose. "Sorry. That sounds like the Week's Good Cause commercial. Like to read about it?"

Thane nodded. Leaning over, she reached into the opened briefcase beside her chair, produced a booklet, and slid it across the table.

"It's all in there. We raised about half a million pounds last year—this year's target is a million."

"Including the Antiques Fair," mused Thane, taking the book-let. "Sarraut reckons it'll be like an Aladdin's Cave road show. And as risky."

"That's why I want the best protection," she grinned. "Like a handy, policeman-shaped lamp."

"And some watertight insurance," suggested Thane pointedly. He paused, seeing Sarraut coming back with the drinks, and asked casually, "Who's handling that?"

"We don't know yet. Peter has contacts. We're hoping some company will donate cover, free of charge." She took the filled glass Sarraut handed her and smiled her thanks. "Subject nor-mal, Ed—but I didn't start it."

"That's a change." The bearded dealer settled in a chair. "Be-fore you ask, I still don't know if I can get back from the States in time. It depends how things are with the business, how many tails I've got to kick."

"But you're going to try?"

"Yes ma'am." He laughed at her concern.

"You're leaving soon?" asked Thane.

"That's right." Sarraut took a gulp from his drink and sat back. "I've spent most of my budget for this trip. Once the rest of the stuff is crated and on its way, I'll follow it over." He frowned around the cocktail bar. "Any idea when that brother of yours will get here, Shona? I don't want to rush you, but—"

"We can start." She reached for the briefcase again. "I can show you the plan of what we've got in mind."

Thane cleared his throat and got to his feet.

"You don't need an audience," he told them. "And I'm due somewhere else."

They said goodbye and he left them. Going out of the hotel, he walked along to his car, got in, and put the key in the starter switch. Then he paused as a car came sweeping along the narrow road, heading towards him. The yellow Jaguar stopped opposite the Ravenwood Hotel. Peter Barry got out from the passenger side, exchanged a quick word with the driver, then closed the door and hurried into the hotel.

The car moved off again, accelerating quickly. As it passed where Thane was sitting, he got a clear glimpse of the driver. A dark-haired, coarse-faced man in his early thirties, thick-set, he wore heavy sunglasses. But his face was one Thane knew from somewhere.

Where was somewhere? Thane puzzled uneasily over that for a full minute, with a definite feeling the answer might be one he wouldn't like. The memory stayed elusive, and though he decided not to forget about it, he gave up, started the car, and set it moving.

Edinburgh Castle closed to visitors at 6 P.M. By the time Thane had found a place to leave his car and had walked to the main gateway a steady stream of visitors had begun to leave. They came down the Castle's long esplanade, talking and joking, taking a few last photographs, passing the statues and memorials to long-ago battles and far-off campaigns.

A kilted soldier from one of the Highland regiments was on sentry duty at the Castle entrance, and two more like him were nearby, keeping a casual eye on the departing visitors. The army still used part of Edinburgh Castle, even if it was a listed Ancient Monument, but sentry duty was mostly ceremonial. One of the soldiers glanced significantly at his watch as Thane went in through the gate, but didn't stop him.

There were plenty of direction signs inside the massive old fortress, some of them pointing towards the Half-Moon Battery. Crossing the old granite cobblestones, Thane remembered the last time he'd been.

He and Mary had brought the children through for the day and it hadn't stopped raining. Even so, they'd enjoyed it, done the full tour—tiny St. Margaret's Chapel, then the Scottish Crown Jewels, the quiet sanctuary of the National War Memorial with its Books of the Fallen, on from there to take a photograph of Tommy grinning in the rain, perched proudly on the barrel of Mons Meg. As far as both Tommy and Kate were concerned, the giant cannon, claimed to have been cast in Belgium when knights in armour still ruled most battlefields, had been the hit of the day.

It had been Tommy's tenth birthday. There had been no hint of any problems then.

Lips tightening at the thought, he increased his stride. The old cannons of the Half-Moon Battery showed ahead, flanking the modern fieldpiece that fired the one o'clock time signal. The ramparts looked deserted, but as he got closer he saw a figure slouched on a bench, bald head glinting in the sunlight.

He crossed over, his footsteps loud on the cobbled way. Malky Darvel didn't look up. He sat with his chin resting against his chest, as if dozing.

Yet his eyes were open, staring unwinkingly at the grey cobbles at his feet. Mouth suddenly dry, Colin Thane touched the man's shoulder.

Very slowly the coffin-maker's body shifted and slumped sideways on the bench. His jacket had fallen open and dark blood had stained a patch of his shirt underneath, a stain centred around a small cut in the material where something very thin and sharp had stabbed through it.

"Damn you," said Thane softly. "I told you not to take risks, didn't I?"

He swallowed hard, took a deep breath, and looked around again. The empty battlements seemed to mock him, to say they'd seen it all before, too many times over the centuries.

Thane lit a cigarette. Then he turned and walked back towards the gate and the army guard detail.

The city didn't matter, the routine was the same. Three minutes after the kilted sergeant of the guard telephoned, the first police car arrived. Until then, even Thane's warrant card hadn't made any difference to the soldier ordered to watch him, a soldier whose rifle and fixed bayonet had stopped being just part of the castle's tourist decoration.

A flustered C.I.D. chief inspector arrived with the second wave, called Thane "sir" a few times, and the rifle and bayonet were put away. The army looked disappointed.

More cars arrived. One held a load of Crime Squad men headed by Francey Dunbar and Malcolm, the lanky duty inspector.

The Edinburgh force sent a chief superintendent with the next wave, as if making certain they got the balance right in terms of rank. Thane knew him. His name was Allison and they'd once been on a firearms course together.

"Bad luck," sympathised Allison. The castle had long since emptied of visitors, none aware of what had happened. A small cluster of soldiers watched, curious, while the police team went about their work. "Didn't touch anything, did you?"

"No," said Thane.

"Sorry." They were standing beside one of the old cannon. Over at the bench, a photographer was still clicking away with his camera with a police surgeon patiently waiting his turn. Behind them were the other specialists and, last in line, the driver of the mortuary wagon. "Well, he was found by a visitor, as far as any press release is concerned."

"Thanks," said Thane. He'd told Allison most of the story, the part that mattered anyway. His eyes strayed again to the bench. "I shouldn't have used him."

"Hindsight's a hell of a clever thing," said Allison. He shrugged. "I'd have done the same. That's the job, isn't it? Use what you've got, the best way you can."

The man moved away, to be replaced by Francey Dunbar. Sober-faced, hands shoved deep into the pockets of his suede jacket, Dunbar sucked an edge of his drooping moustache for a moment, saying nothing.

"Next time someone tries to warn me, make me listen," said Thane bitterly. "I talked Darvel into this."

"Not into getting killed. He must have got careless." His sergeant grimaced, then gestured to the waiting knot of Crime Squad men. "When we heard, Inspector Malcolm grabbed anyone he had to spare. Do we pitch in with the local mob?"

"Any help they want. But it's their murder." Thane realised there was someone missing. "Where's Sandra?"

"She'd gone out. Something about having a date later, wanting to get organised." Dunbar frowned. "Maybe I could find her."

Thane shook his head. "Leave her for now." He drew a deep breath. "How about that Clanmore list?"

"No names that ring bells," admitted Dunbar. "I'm still working on it."

Time seemed to crawl past, but at last they had the police surgeon's initial report. Malky Darvel had died only a short time before Thane's arrival. He had been killed by a single stab wound which had penetrated deep between his ribs, straight into the heart.

"The guess is something long, thin and rounded, maybe a sharpened bicycle spoke. None of our regular Edinburgh villains have favoured that style lately." Chief Superintendent Allison raised a quizzical eyebrow at Thane. "How about your Glasgow flock?"

"No." Thane could only think of one man, and he was firmly out of circulation, would be for at least another ten years.

"Well, somebody had to follow him up here," mused Allison. "Maybe they were sitting together, even talking, then—zap." He rubbed the back of his neck. "Your man would hardly twitch. If there were other folk around, they wouldn't notice a thing."

"You've got a problem," said Thane.

"I'd be happier if you made that 'we.'" Allison gave Thane a slight grin. "I'm not too proud to ask for help. Can your local Crime Squad boys pitch in?"

"I was hoping you'd ask," admitted Thane.

"I'm thinking of antiques land," said Allison. "A full backtrack on where Darvel might have been." He gestured around. "We forget the niceties, right? You've got the whole damned jigsaw, this is one of the corners."

They stopped talking. Two policemen were helping the mortuary driver load Darvel's body into a basket shell. As they carried their burden away, Allison sighed.

"What about his family?"

Thane knew what he meant. "Telling them is my job. I owe him that."

"Your decision." Allison went a few paces to the edge of the castle ramparts and looked down at the city below. "Somebody has to do it. Aye, somebody always has."

It was still about another hour before Thane could leave. It was going to be a glorious sunset, and the castle sat like a black medieval tapestry in stone against a red-gold sky as he walked out past the army sentries and headed for his car.

As he got in behind the wheel, footsteps hurried towards him. Francey Dunbar arrived almost out of breath, and looked in.

"Want me along?" he asked.

Thane shook his head.

Dunbar didn't argue. "What about tomorrow?"

Thane shrugged. "Eight A.M., my office. We'll take it from there."

Dunbar stood back and the Ford moved off with a vicious squeal of rubber.

It was three hours later, not far short of midnight, when Colin Thane got home. It had clouded overhead and there was a thin drizzle of rain in the air, as if the weather matched his mood.

Malky Darvel's wife and son had tried hard but the news of his murder had still meant initial, staring disbelief, then tears and bewilderment. He had hoped it might help them to know the little coffin-maker had been working for the police . . . and he had kept it at "the police," not for Superintendent Colin Thane.

It hadn't. Maybe it would later. And neither of them knew anything about Darvel's contacts in the grey half-world of antiques faking.

Thane left the car outside his house and went in. Mary had stayed up, waiting for him.

"I've heard," she told him before he could say a word. "Francey Dunbar phoned from Edinburgh. He thought I'd better know." She took his hands in her own for a moment, knowing her man. "How did his family take it?"

He shook his head, went over to their drinks cupboard, brought out the bottle of whisky he'd bought the previous night for Phil Moss's visit, and poured himself a stiff measure.

"I kept some supper. I reckoned you'd need it."

Mary brought the food through while he drank the whisky. As she laid the tray on a table, he swallowed the last of it. There was something else on his mind.

"What happened with Tommy?" he asked.

"It'll keep." She pointed to the tray. "Food first."

The slab of meat pie had been kept warm in the kitchen oven a little too long to be at its best. But he ate it hungrily, followed it with some biscuits and cheese washed down with coffee, then sat back feeling considerably more human.

"Now," he insisted. "Tommy."

"I don't want him wakened," she warned. "It—well, it isn't so important. I just blew my top at the time."

She went over to the sideboard, opened the top cutlery drawer, and came back.

"I found this in his room."

Colin Thane stared at the twisted piece of metal she placed in front of him. It had been a table fork. The handle had been removed and the four prongs bent outward at precise angles, each ending with an inward curving point. He picked it up, examined it again, then looked at her.

"It's not one of our best," she said almost defensively, misunderstanding his silence. "But why did he have to do that?"

Thane had to moisten his lips. "Did you ask him?"

She nodded. "He said he used it to try to mend something on his bike. That he couldn't find a screwdriver."

Thane looked at the twisted fork again. He knew exactly what it was. Tommy had made himself a "jigger" tool, one of the latest and more sophisticated items developed by the juvenile crime league.

The four prongs of the fork duplicated the special key needed to open pay telephone coin boxes or the locks on prepayment electric meters. The first of them was credited to the notion of a bored inmate at a juvenile detention centre near London. Ever since, the "jiggers" had been turning up in different parts of the country. Every police force had sent out an intelligence sheet about them.

"It's not one of our best forks," repeated Mary. "Even so—"

"I know." He couldn't tell her, not yet. Not until he had time to think, to find out more about what was going on. He drew a deep breath. "Tomorrow night. Let's talk about it then."

Her lips tightened slightly and he knew she was puzzled. But she nodded.

A little later, as they started to get ready for bed, Thane made an excuse about needing something for the morning and went out to the garage. Their old station wagon filled most of the space inside, but he switched on the overhead light and went to the workbench.

Bending down, he reached into the space between the bench and the concrete floor and brought out a small wooden box, the lid fastened by a small, cheap padlock.

The box was Tommy's. He had had it for years and called it his "treasure chest." He had bought the padlock with his pocket money after finding his sister rummaging through the box.

The padlock was locked. Thane laid the battered box on the workbench, drew a deep breath, and found a piece of stiff wire.

It took him about a minute to master the padlock and remove it. He hesitated again, then opened the lid.

He looked down at an old catapult, a police whistle, a broken watch, and all the other bits and pieces that Tommy had accumulated. There was something wrapped in a grubby scrap of cloth underneath.

He lifted it out, heard the jingle of metal, and unwrapped the little bundle.

A collection of car keys, all different, tied together on a loop of wire, glinted in the light from the bare bulb overhead.

For a long moment Thane could only stare at them. Then, feeling sick, he put the keys in his pocket, locked the box again, and put it back in its hiding place.

When he went back into the house he said nothing. But later, lying awake in bed, Mary asleep beside him, he stared at the ceiling.

The only thing he knew for sure was that he needed help on this one. That no sensible parent would go in and tackle it alone.

Particularly when that parent was a cop.

CHAPTER 6

Even the dog was still asleep next morning when Colin Thane rose and dressed. He went downstairs, made a mug of instant coffee, then drank it and smoked a cigarette while he looked out at the dawn light and the fine drizzle of rain still falling.

He left at 6:20 A.M., the house still silent, got into his car, and started off for the rendezvous Maggie Fyffe had made for him with the mysterious voice on the telephone. The damp streets were still almost empty of traffic apart from an occasional half-empty bus or clattering milk-delivery truck.

It was only a twenty-minute drive to Shields Road underground station and the meeting had been set for seven. But it was the kind of situation where he preferred to be early, to take no chances. Lying just south of the river, in an area of factory buildings, warehouses and old tenements, Shields Road station was about as desolate an early-morning meeting place as he could imagine.

The thought stayed as he reached the place. Demolition work had left the underground station totally isolated in a long, muddy strip of waste ground. On the other side of the road were warehouse buildings, still shut and empty.

Bouncing the Ford over the kerb and onto the waste ground, Thane stopped it close to the small brick building which was the entry and exit point for what lay below. It was open for business, and as he got out of the car the ground vibrated beneath his feet and he heard the rumble of a train pulling in. As it pulled away again, two workmen emerged from the station and trudged past him through the drizzle, heading for the start of another day.

He looked around. There was no one else in sight and the only other vehicle on the waste ground was an old van, lying about fifty yards from the station building. Walking over, he felt the radiator. It was cold and the van body was dripping wet as if it had been there all night.

Thane went back to the Crime Squad car, got in, and smoked his second cigarette of the day. The problem he'd left at home kept coming into his mind, but he felt as much as heard another underground train arrive and depart. This time a few sleepy-eyed passengers emerged from the station and went past. An occasional vehicle hissed along the wet road. Then a car drew up and he tensed. But it stopped just long enough to let a girl tumble out of the passenger seat and hurry into the station.

Her hair was a mess and she was wearing a party dress covered by what looked like a borrowed raincoat. Stubbing his cigarette in the dashboard ashtray, Thane grinned. Where she'd been and what she was going to have to explain to someone gave room for some guesswork.

At 7 A.M. exactly he got out of the car again and took position outside the station entrance. Coat collar turned up against the drizzle, he eventually felt the ground shake again, then watched as another handful of passengers came up the stairway from the tunnel below. Totally ignoring him, they walked past and went their separate ways.

Another couple of minutes passed. Traffic on the road was gradually beginning to increase. He sighed, shifted his feet impatiently, then heard a deliberate, throat-clearing noise behind him.

He turned. A little bantam of a man in working clothes and wearing a cloth cap had emerged from the station entrance and was standing there, a wary expression on his thin, unshaven face.

"Good morning," said Thane.

"Is it?" Hands deep in the pockets of his black donkey jacket, the little man gave a grunt. "Not for me, at this hour. An' I don't make a habit of this."

"You're from Harald Street?" asked Thane directly.

The man's eyes widened slightly, then he nodded. "You helped a girl a couple o' days back. My youngest—"

"I remember," said Thane. "And I heard there was some sorting out later. Your business, not mine."

"All three o' them got banjoed enough so they won't forget." The little stranger gave a broken-toothed grin, then let it fade. "I've a name for you, mister. Someone Anna Marshton knew well—if you want it."

Thane nodded. "I want."

"Goldie Boyd." A pair of sharp eyes watched for reaction. "Know him?"

"Yes." He stiffened in surprise. Goldie Boyd was a professional, tough and ruthless with it. In his mid-thirties, he had won the nickname "Goldie" from the small fortune in gold fillings in his teeth. His official criminal record wasn't spectacular, early conviction for armed robbery and another for possessing explosives. But every cop who had ever come in contact with Boyd knew he was a grafter, a man who ran tight, well-planned operations—and showed little mercy to anyone who let him down. Thane drew a deep breath. "I wouldn't have put Anna in Goldie's league."

"They were kinfolk—second cousins or somethin'." The little man shrugged his indifference. "The word around is she'd been workin' for him. Not steady, just to help out."

"That happens." Thane had only once been involved with Goldie Boyd and the case had got nowhere. But he knew Boyd ran a very small regular team, then recruited and discarded the rest as he needed. "What was Anna into?"

"No idea, mister."

"But maybe that's why she was killed?" persisted Thane.

The little man scowled. "I didn't say that—hell, I don't know. I'm givin' you a name, that's all. Squarin' for the way you helped my youngest." He pulled out a cheap pocket watch and frowned at it. "That's it. I work over on the north side, an' if I'm late some nosey basket might wonder why."

"I could use another name—yours," said Thane.

"Mine? No way." The reply came with a sardonic grin. "I've enough problems. But you know what that kid of mine was carryin'?"

Thane nodded. "And bookies don't pay out twice."

"Right," said the little man cheerfully. He broke off, listened, then added, "Don't come lookin' for me. Because I've never seen you."

He turned quickly and hurried back down the steps of the underground station. Moments later the ground vibrated with the noise of an approaching train. It stopped below, Thane heard the muffled sigh of opening doors, then they closed again and the train rumbled off.

Goldie Boyd. Thane moved aside as a small group of newly arrived passengers came out of the station entrance, then stayed where he was, ignoring the continuing drizzle.

There was no particular king in Glasgow's underworld. Anyone who claimed that title had a habit of ending up dead in a ditch or at least behind bars. But Boyd certainly rated. If he didn't make the top rank of the criminal elite, he wasn't far behind them. His name had been linked with more than one unsolved killing.

If Goldie Boyd was the Glasgow end—

The thought stopped there. Thane stared across the waste ground, at the parked van which had been there when he'd arrived. The rear door was open. Francey Dunbar was already coming out and coming towards him, and Joe Felix was at his heels.

"Do we pick him up, sir?" asked Dunbar briskly as he arrived. He grinned at Thane's expression. "Boyd, I mean. It sounds good."

"How the hell do you know, and what the hell are you doing here?" exploded Thane, bewildered.

"Maggie tipped us," said Dunbar unabashed. He gestured at Felix. "Joe dumped the van here last night, then we got here about six and settled in." He shivered in the drizzle. "Damned uncomfortable it was too."

"But it wouldn't look good if our boss got duffed up, would it?" said Felix almost apologetically. "So—uh—Francey and I thought we'd better be around."

Thane considered him suspiciously. "And the rest of it?"

Felix looked pleased. He pointed up towards the flat roof of the underground station.

"A remote-control microphone up there, sir—brand-new, multi-segment head, medium-range pickup. I've been wanting a chance to use it. Then once you got talking, I used a gun mike from the van." He beamed enthusiastically. "We've got it all on tape."

"In case of problems," said Francey Dunbar, beginning to eye Thane warily.

"When it's set to music, let me know," Thane told them. "Who decided I needed a pair of nursemaids?"

"Well, Maggie thought—" Dunbar stopped it there, looked sheepish, and tried again. "You could have walked into something."

"Next time you'll walk into my boot." Thane still felt indignant at their protective attitude. The drizzle was getting heavier and he could feel some of it running down the back of his neck, which didn't help. "Where's the nearest place we can get breakfast?"

Dunbar frowned. "How about Goldie Boyd?"

"He'll keep till we've more to go on." Thane meant it, but there was also something nagging at the back of his mind, partly eluding him, yet to do with Boyd. "I said breakfast. Or do you want to stay and drown in this wet?"

It was about an hour later when they reached the Crime Squad headquarters building. Sandra Craig was already there, waiting in the duty room.

"About last night—" she began penitently as soon as she saw Thane.

"Forget it." He knew what was troubling her, but also felt a wisp of amusement. Detective Constable Craig looked as though she'd had a long, exhausting night. There were dark patches under her eyes and her red hair straggled like an unkempt bush. "You hadn't a crystal ball. You were due time off."

"Even so—" she tried again.

He shook his head. "When did you get back—or should I ask?"

She winced. "We ended up in a jazz club. Can I leave it there?"

Thane decided he'd better.

There was already a telex message waiting from Edinburgh, an overnight update on the continuing search for Malky Darvel's killer. But it made bleak reading. Despite plenty of effort, things were no further forward than when he had left.

Other people had decided on an early start that morning. Commander Hart arrived a few minutes later. Almost immediately he summoned Thane through.

"Sit down, Colin." The morning papers, still unopened, lay in front of him. That was unusual enough to show he was worried. Hart normally began his day with a fast check through the comic strips, and serious reading came later. He eyed Thane stonily across the desk. "Got yourself into the manure a bit, haven't you?"

Thane flushed, though he'd expected it. "It looks that way."

"It *is* that way," said Hart. "All right, so far the bottom line isn't exactly a success story. I'm not faulting you—not yet, anyway." He paused, laid both hands on the desk, and leaned forward a little. "But I want to know how things stand now—your version, not what I'll read on the report sheets."

Thane told him. It didn't take long, and at the end of it the Squad commander sat silent for a moment, a frown deepening the lines on his thin face.

"You're widening the insurance company checks?"

Thane nodded.

"If we had an idea, a notion even, about their next target—" Hart stopped it there. Then, a more hopeful note in his voice, he asked, "What about Goldie Boyd?"

"I'd like something more to go on," said Thane. "Even if he is in on it, he's not running the show."

"No." Hart nodded reluctantly. "Your way then, for the moment. If you need extra help, ask. That's all." He looked up as Thane rose. "Except—"

"Sir?"

"That man, Darvel," said Hart softly. "You didn't kill him—they did. Remember that."

Back out in the duty room, he gathered his small team around him again.

"We're not being leaned on yet," he told them. "But we haven't won any medals. We're going to have to push on fast, with anything we've got—including those insurance company lists."

Francey Dunbar gave a groan. "Computer land."

Thane nodded. "Work it dry. If you hit problems or you need advice, find some outside expert—a university boffin, someone like that."

"You've got one," said Sandra Craig.

"Who?" Thane glanced at her, puzzled.

"Peter Barry." She saw his surprise and nodded. "He's into computer technology in a big way, the programming and software side."

Thane swallowed. Francey Dunbar and Joe Felix looked equally blank.

"Who says?" asked Felix.

"Ed Sarraut—he told me last night." She was puzzled. "I thought you knew."

"I do now," said Thane. "I thought he ran a business consultancy outfit."

Sandra nodded. "He does—computer-based office systems."

"How good is he at it?"

"Top line." She paused uneasily. "That's why the Ransom Trust people think they'll have no problems with insurance cover for their Antiques Fair. He helped set up computer programming systems for some of the Scottish companies."

Francey Dunbar swore under his breath. Thane said nothing. He was thinking of a girl with long, dark hair driving up to

Drum Lodge. Then of the stranger he'd seen deliver Peter Barry to that Edinburgh hotel, a stranger whose face still worried him.

"Peter Barry wasn't on the Clanmore list of names," said Dunbar slowly. He rubbed his chin. "But suppose it should have been—"

Thane nodded and glanced at his watch. It was after 9 A.M., time for most business offices to begin stirring.

"Ask," he said. "But don't make waves." As Dunbar crossed to the telephone he switched back to the girl. "Did Sarraut say anything else about Barry—like how they met?"

"It was through Barry's sister. She wanted Ed to help with the Antiques Fair." Sandra Craig's usual confidence was shaken. "But do you really think Barry could be involved? I mean—"

"When I'm handing out clean bills of health I'll tell you," he said explosively. "From now on, remember that."

Tight-lipped, she nodded. Joe Felix glared in Thane's direction but said nothing.

"All right." His anger subsided as quickly as it had flared and he was already regretting it, knowing she'd just happened to be handy. "So it isn't a happy day—for any of us. What about this collection of antiques Sarraut is taking back to the States? Is it big enough to matter?"

"To us?" She understood but shook her head. "Most of it, all the heavy stuff, is already on its way by sea. The rest will go air freight, but there's not a lot of it."

"Low bulk, high value?" asked Felix.

"He says no, not by trade standards. Maybe sixty thousand dollars' worth—fragile items like china and porcelain, old silver, that kind of thing." She shrugged. "It's not enough, is it?"

"No," agreed Thane. He gave her a wry, lopsided smile. "But it helps to know."

She thawed, grinned, and produced a chocolate bar. As she bit a chunk from it, Francey Dunbar finished his telephone call and came back.

"I got Talbot at Clanmore Mutual," he announced, perching himself on the desk, an odd gleam in his eyes. "That's after I battled past his secretary—and she's damned near bulletproof."

"Save that for your memoirs," said Thane. "What about Barry?"

"Peter Barry was a consultant on the original Clanmore think-tank committee that set up their system—and the security coding." The silver chain on Dunbar's wrist clinked as he grinned and rubbed his chin. "Would you believe this? None of that committee are on our list because their names weren't given to the computer—Barry said it wasn't necessary."

"As easy as that?" Thane almost groaned aloud.

"Uh-huh." Dunbar hadn't finished. "Barry still calls around now and again, to keep an eye on how things are going. The Clanmore mob think he's wonderful."

"Don't we all?" asked Thane bitterly. "Check out Barry and his sister. Get Edinburgh to help on it. The full treatment, Francey. But I don't want him to catch a hint of it, not yet."

Dunbar nodded. "What about this end—Goldie Boyd?"

"I'll take care of that." Thane put a cigarette between his lips and let it dangle there, unlit, looking at the three faces opposite him. "Barry and his sister may seem clean enough, with their Ransom Trust connections. But charity can begin at home, can't it?"

There were several ways he could have gone searching for information about Goldie Boyd. Thane chose the most direct, the one that bypassed official channels, that came down to relying on whom he knew.

Partly because it was the quickest. Partly because he had another, totally different mission which mattered at least as much.

Taking the Ford, he drove into the city, and ten minutes later he had turned into the parking lot behind Strathclyde Police Headquarters. He abandoned the car in one of the official visitor slots, nodded to the uniformed man on guard duty, and went into the headquarters building.

It was sheer bad luck that one of the first people he met inside was Chief Inspector Fred Kiesen. The Divisional man came striding along the same corridor, and the scowl on his heavy face deepened in suspicion as he saw Thane.

"What the hell brings you here?" demanded Kiesen in his hoarse whisper of a voice. "If it's the Anna Marshton business—"

"You stick to your side of the fence, I'll stick to mine," Thane told him curtly. "Get off my back, Fred. I've enough problems."

"I heard. Somebody died on you through in Edinburgh, right?" Kiesen sniffed derisively. "I'd call that careless."

"Would you?" Thane grabbed him by the shoulder, and glared at him for a moment. "Fred, don't push your luck. I mean it, understand?"

Kiesen nodded, and backed away a step as Thane let him go.

"Before you go, Chief Inspector." Thane dropped his voice to a flat monotone. "You said Anna Marshton. You're the one with the theory it was a sex killing. Found that other girl yet—the one in the car?"

"No," admitted Kiesen. He saw Thane's expression, swallowed, and corrected himself. "No, sir."

Thane turned on his heel and left him.

In his new headquarters liaison job, Phil Moss had a small office to himself, one of the rooms located just outside the area every Glasgow cop knew as the Holy City—the short length of carpeted corridor where every door belonged to at least an assistant chief constable.

In his shirtsleeves, his tie undone, a mug of coffee at his elbow, he looked up from his desk and smiled as Thane came in.

"Welcome to wonderland." He gestured at the litter of papers on his desk. "I'm wondering what to do about this, that, and every other damned thing. Grab a chair and sit down."

Thane closed the door, took a chair, and settled opposite him.

"In about the Anna Marshton business?" asked Moss. He pointed towards the wall. "A.C.C. Crime has just had Fred Kiesen in. He's getting nowhere."

"I saw him." Thane took a deep breath. "That's not why I'm here, Phil. It's—well, it's Tommy."

"*Your* Tommy?" Moss's mouth opened in surprise, then he took a quick gulp of coffee. "What's happened?"

"These are part of it." Thane reached into his pocket, brought out the bundle of car keys which had been lying there since he left home, and laid them on the desk. "There's more."

"Hell." Moss laid the mug down carefully. Picking up the car keys, he fingered them for a moment. "What's the rest of it?"

Thane told him. It wasn't easy, even with Moss. But at least, when he'd finished, he felt slightly better.

"Car keys any kid can get his hands on," said Moss. He chewed a thin lip for a moment. "But a homemade jigger key— any notions there?"

Thane shook his head. "No."

"How about Mary?"

"I've got to tell her," said Thane. "She has a right to know. But it's what to do afterwards."

"Yes." Moss whistled tunelessly through his teeth for a moment. "You need someone else to do the real dirty work. Does Tommy know the car keys are gone?"

"I don't think so. He may look for them this afternoon, after school." Thane shrugged helplessly. "Phil, I don't think he's in deep, but—"

"Leave it," said Moss. "Tell Mary, but do nothing, say nothing as far as he's concerned—not yet. Okay?" He hefted the keys in his hand, then opened a drawer of his desk and tossed them in. "And I do it my way. Free hand—agreed?"

Thane nodded.

"Right." Moss gave him a slight, unexpected grin. "Thanks. For asking me, I mean. And if a certain young gentleman ends up with his tail in a sling, he's still on my Christmas list." He rose and gestured at his desk top. "Now do two things for me, will you? Try and forget about it till you see Mary—and get the hell out of here. I've work to do."

Thane walked away from the little office with at least a semblance of the usual spring in his stride and his thoughts a lot clearer than they'd been for some hours.

Criminal Intelligence was two floors down. In appearance, it was a large, open-plan office area filled with filing cabinets, flickering VDU screens linked to the police computer network, and surprisingly few desks. The staff in Criminal Intelligence were long-service men, experts at their job of sifting gossip, matching it to rumour, swooping on the occasional apparently unrelated hard fact in some beat cop's report. What they knew, what they produced, would have shattered the confidence of many a criminal—and plenty of other people who had skated close to the brink but would never have guessed they might be on file.

The man Thane wanted was at one of the desks, half hidden behind a screen of greenery. Sam Paxton was a detective sergeant, fair-haired, quiet, and held the Queen's Police Medal for bravery. Tomato plants were his pride and joy. He wore a surgical corset and always would, a souvenir of his last day working outside when a drunken ned armed with a bayonet tried very hard to disembowel him.

"What do you think of them?" he asked cheerfully, pointing to the plants. "Two weeks ago they were dying, then I brought them in here. Cigarette smoke, coffee dregs and a few kind words—that's all they needed."

"That goes for most of us," said Thane. "Sam, I need some help."

"Sideways style?" Paxton grinned as Thane nodded, reached under the desk, and thumped a charity box on the wood. "It'll cost you."

"It always does." There was a Ransom Trust wheelchair symbol on the box. Without comment, Thane fed some change into the slot. "I want what you've got on Goldie Boyd."

"No problem." Paxton got up, headed for the nearest VDU screen, used it, then moved over to the filing cabinets. When he came back, he slapped down a folder. "Boyd, Roy Eastam, otherwise Goldie. Be my guest."

Goldie Boyd's photograph was on the first page. He had a thin face with high cheekbones and a receding hairline and his lips were closed tight, hiding the dental work which had won him his nickname. Underneath, his basic biography was laid out in *Who's Who* style. Thane leafed on, through pages that covered the man's known or suspected activities, even his drinking habits and women he'd been involved with.

"Got him in mind for something?" asked Sam Paxton.

"I'm hoping." Thane passed a note that a Marine Division cop had spotted Boyd having a winter week in a five-star Majorcan hotel. The cop had been in a no-star *hostel* down the road. Then he found what he wanted, half a dozen names under the heading Current Associates. "Can you pull these heroes for me?"

Paxton nodded. It took a little longer this time, and when he returned he had only four folders.

"Forget the other two," said Paxton. "They're doing time down south." He spread the folders like a fan on his desk. "It's still a useful little team. Willie Laird and big Tam Amos have been breaking and entering since they could walk. Mule Pearson is a damned good locks man and Shug Gordon is—well, you always need someone to do what he's told."

"I know him." Thane pushed Shug Gordon's folder aside, started to reach for the one marked Laird, then hesitated. Suddenly, knowing he had to be right, he opened the Mule Pearson folder.

The photograph of a dark-haired, coarse-faced man stared up at him. The same man he'd seen driving for Peter Barry in Edinburgh—

"Got something?" asked Paxton, coming closer.

Thane nodded, hardly trusting himself to say anything. Mule Pearson, a man with a string of convictions for theft and robbery, a technician when it came to locks and security systems, meant a positive tie between Goldie Boyd and Peter Barry.

Boyd and Barry. Their names sounded like a music hall act. But put them together, blend Boyd's ruthless style of operation with Barry's knowledge of antiques and computers, and the result could be formidable.

Was formidable. The long string of robberies, two murders, and a fringe of lesser crimes—with the big one, the one it was really all about, still to come. He moistened his lips.

"Sam, one more name. Peter Barry. He's Edinburgh, a computer boffin—the odds are he's clean. Try it, will you?"

"Sure." Paxton lingered a moment. "What about this bunch?"

"Leave them."

Paxton ambled away and began tapping a VDU keyboard. Nobody ever admitted knowing just what percentage of the population had something about them stored between police computer memory banks and related files. Democracy wasn't supposed to work that way. But one Strathclyde region chief constable's annual report had let it slip that in his area alone 170,000 "case disposal" details were being fed into the system each year.

If Peter Barry had ever done anything more criminal than collect a parking ticket, had even drifted across the fringe of an investigation, then it was on record somewhere.

It took seventy seconds, a good fifteen of them because Sam Paxton knew there was more than one way to spell a name like Barry. Then he came back with a sad expression and a narrow printout slip in one hand.

"This could be him. Obstructing the police and disorderly conduct six years ago—something to do with an antinuclear demo. Fined twenty pounds. He'd been picked up a couple of times before on other protest marches, but that was his first time in court. That's all we've got."

"Forget it." Thane hid his disappointment. But he hadn't really expected much. It would have been too easy that way. He nodded at the phone on Paxton's desk. "Mind?"

"Go ahead."

Paxton had another customer waiting, a woman inspector who was Fraud Squad. As he went to meet her, Thane lifted the receiver, dialled the Scottish Crime Squad number, and got through to Francey Dunbar.

"I've some news for you," said Dunbar in the toneless voice he kept for when things were beginning to happen. "So far, we've got three more insurance outfits where friend Barry has had something to do with their computer layout. Do I get a prize if we get to five?"

"At least a free haircut," promised Thane. "How about the Edinburgh end?"

"They're working on it—nothing back yet," reported Dunbar. "Uh—you're not surprised?"

"Not now," said Thane flatly. "The Goldie Boyd story stands up." He heard his sergeant give a soft whistle at the other end of the line and smiled to himself. "We're in business, Francey. Tell Edinburgh it's now a surveillance watch on Barry—and I want the same on his sister."

"How about Goldie Boyd?" asked Dunbar. "Pickup time?"

"Not yet," said Thane. "We need more—when we nail them, I want them to stay nailed and I want the team."

He told Dunbar the names on the Criminal Intelligence files, then hung up. Before he left, he asked Sam Paxton to send a detailed teleprint feed to the Scottish Crime Squad.

Minutes later, on his way out of the building, he saw Phil Moss in the distance. He could have hailed him but didn't. Moss would do his level best as far as Tommy was concerned, without any reminders. For the moment, though he wished things were different, Colin Thane knew he had to leave it that way.

Leave it, with a silent prayer things would really work out.

He had one thing more to do before he returned. It was a forlorn hope, and it meant another crosstown drive out to Malky Darvel's coffin workshop.

The Maldar Wood Products building looked deserted when he parked outside. But when he knocked on the main door it was opened by the elderly workman he'd seen on his previous visit. The man recognised him and let him in.

"On your own?" asked Thane.

The man nodded. He had sawdust on his overalls and a coffin different from the others around, the wood a fine-grained oak, was taking shape on a bench in the middle of the workshop.

"Mrs. Darvel gave me the okay," the man said with gruff embarrassment. "Malky used to say he'd want somethin' better than our regular line." He paused. "So what do you want?"

"A key to the back room," Thane told him bluntly. "Got one?"

Stony-faced, the workman reached into an overall pocket and handed Thane a single key on a cheap plastic fob.

"You won't find much, mister," he said. "If it mattered, Malky kept it to himself—and in his head."

Thane left him, went through the maze of stacked coffins, and unlocked the door at the rear. Switching on the light, he stepped into the room where Malky Dunbar had practiced his special art.

The waiting, half-completed antiques made him almost shiver, as if Malky Darvel was by his side again. Tight-lipped, he headed for the tool-bench and started searching.

There was not as much as a scrap of paper to hint who Darvel knew outside or worked with. He gave up at last, locked the room again, and tried the little general office. The Malder Wood Products records were there, scattered around in an untidy confusion.

But nothing else, not the smallest link to connect the dead man with his other trade. Going out into the main workshop, where the elderly man was hand-sandpapering one side of the oak coffin to an almost satin sheen.

"Like I tol' you, right?" The sandpapering rhythm hardly faltered as he took the key from Thane. "Malky always played it safe."

"Not yesterday," said Thane grimly.

"Aye," said the workman. He shrugged, then reached for a fresh piece of sandpaper. "Bad, that. Who the hell would want to die in Edinburgh?"

It was still a long way off noon as Colin Thane drove the north-south motorway route back to the S.C.S. headquarters. There was a gusting wind, strong enough to make itself felt as it caught at the car, but the sky was clear of cloud and the temperature was rising. Eyes narrowed against the bright sunlight, he was south of the river when the Ford's radio murmured his call sign.

He answered, steering one-handed.

"Return to base," came the operator's calm, unemotional voice. "Command priority, and state estimated arrival time."

"Four minutes." He signed off, puzzled, and shoved down on the accelerator. Command priority meant the message came direct from Jack Hart, and the squad commander didn't use the prefix lightly.

There was no sign of particular urgency when he reached the Training Area. The Dog Branch had a class under way as usual on one of the fields beside the driveway, and a bunch of cadets were being marched around as if they were needed by the Brigade of Guards.

It was different in the parking area behind the S.C.S. building. He saw other cars had been brought in. Two more were arriving as he stopped and got out.

And someone was keeping a close eye on the monitor screens. When he went in, Commander Hart met him near Maggie Fyffe's desk while a worried Francey Dunbar hovered near.

"The kettle has started boiling," said Hart. He beckoned Dunbar forward. "Tell him, Sergeant."

"Peter Barry is on the move." Dunbar took a quick gnaw at a stray straggle of his moustache, and managed a sideways glance at Hart. "It looks like it's for real. Can't be anything else."

"God," said Hart, "never mind the analysis-in-depth bit, Francey. Just bloody tell it."

"Sir. Barry arrived at his office in Edinburgh with a suitcase this morning. He left after about an hour." Dunbar shrugged. "All his secretary knows is that he is on some kind of a business trip to London and he'll be back sometime next week."

"Go on." Thane's eyes narrowed. "How about the surveillance team?"

Dunbar shook his head. "It happened before they moved in."

"Then how do we know?" asked Thane.

"Luck," admitted Dunbar. "That Crime Prevention Officer

you fixed for Shona Barry got things mixed up, thought it was the brother he had to see. So he looked in at Barry's office this morning, asked for him, and got told the tale—and he walked out as the surveillance team rolled up."

"That's it," said Hart. Hands clasped together, he rubbed them slowly. "Edinburgh says Barry's sister is still around, behaving normally. But if we've put the rest together right way around, then—"

Thane nodded. "Whatever he's planning, it's under way." He guessed what was coming. "You want to grab Goldie Boyd's team?"

"We've got to," said Hart. "It's that, or risk waiting till God knows what happens." He shook his head. "That's no choice. We're maybe too damned late already, but we can try. And if we get even one of them—"

He left the rest unsaid. But they knew exactly what he meant.

It was a maximum effort. In the next hour, carloads of Crime Squad officers raided fourteen addresses in different parts of Glasgow. They had a cover story which involved an armed holdup in Greenock, they picked up one army deserter wanted for serious assault and two smash-and-grab men who had jumped bail. Shug Gordon's sister also had to be brought in after she made a determined attempt to alter a detective constable's face with a broken bottle.

But Goldie Boyd and his team of four had vanished. Beaten them by a matter of a few hours at most, if the very little help they got from anyone could be believed.

Half an hour later, an anonymous telephone tip-off sent two cars racing to a fifteenth address where Tam Amos was supposed to be located.

It was a narrow street of derelict tenements close to the heart of dockland. And it was a deliberate ambush. As the men left the cars a sudden deluge of bricks, bottles and stones rained down on them from the windows above. Figures appeared in doorways just long enough to hurl other missiles—and as the startled officers dived for the cover of their cars again, one of them yelling an emergency code twenty-one into his radio, a petrol bomb exploded in the roadway.

Rushed in by van and using police dogs, a Support Group Squad moved in and cleaned out the derelict tenements. They brought out the ringleader and two others, all in their teens, all street-gang regulars.

It had nothing to do with Tam Amos. But a detective constable was in hospital with a broken arm, two more had been injured, and one of the Crime Squad cars had to be towed away.

They'd lost it. By three o'clock in the afternoon it had to be admitted, accepted. Commander Hart was in a sombre mood when Thane answered a summons to his office.

"Maybe there isn't too much damage done," said Hart. He indicated a message form on his desk. "Greenock have just picked up three local villains for that armed holdup. We can have the word spread around, make it sound like we've stopped being interested in Boyd's bunch." Looking tired, older than usual, he rubbed his chin. "Still, they're not going to show. About all we're left with is Barry's sister."

Thane had been waiting for that. There had been activity in several directions over the past few hours. The Edinburgh branch had scraped together a reasonably comprehensive background on both Peter Barry and his sister. During the lunch hour, when Barry's unsuspecting secretary had been out, his small office had been thoroughly searched.

The two detectives who had done that wouldn't file any official report. But they had photographed page after page of Peter Barry's desk diary, whenever they saw blank pages or the scribbled entry "out of town."

More often than not, the dates covered the periods when one or other of the antiques robberies had taken place. In the same way, squeezing every contact available, using every favour owed or threatening thunderbolts of retribution, some of the Glasgow

S.C.S. men had established that Goldie Boyd's team had simi-
larly vanished around those dates.

The clincher had come in about the same time. Barry had told
his secretary he was catching a plane from Edinburgh airport.
His car, a black B.M.W., was in the airport carpark. His suitcase
wasn't aboard.

But no one answering Peter Barry's description had been on
any flight out.

"Well?" Hart asked it again. "Barry's sister. What do we do
about her?"

They looked at each other in silence for a moment, both knowing that, whatever they did, there was a gamble involved.

"I'll drive through and talk to her," said Thane slowly. He got
to his feet, then added, "How much I tell her is something I'll
have to play by ear."

"Do that." Hart gave a grimace. "If anything happens at this
end you'll hear—believe me."

Thane left him and went through to the duty room. It had
seen hustle and activity earlier, but now it was back to normal,
almost deserted. He saw Joe Felix at his desk.

"Where's Francey?" asked Thane.

"Uh—out," said Felix vaguely, looking up from a tangle of
electronic circuits he was either taking apart or putting together.
"He had a phone call from somewhere and said to tell you he
had to go." He reached for a tiny screwdriver. "It's probably
Federation business."

"Now?" Thane glared at him.

"He's the Squad delegate," Felix reminded him.

"I've heard," said Thane acidly. The latest Police Federation
claim included a demand for better shift allowances and over-
time. But their interest and membership stopped short of superintendent rank. "When our union hero gets back, tell him I've
gone through to Edinburgh." He looked around. "Where's
Sandra?"

"Gone to get something to eat," said Felix. Then he brightened and pointed. "Here she comes."

Thane turned. Detective Constable Sandra Craig came walking towards them, looking her usual cool, slim and attractive self and munching at a meat pie. In her free hand, she was carrying a paper grocery bag.

"Work," Thane told her. "We're going to Edinburgh." He pointed to the grocery bag. "Forget the emergency rations—you won't need them."

"No, sir." She dumped the grocery bag on Felix's desk, and gave Thane an innocent smile. "The way you drive, who'd want them?"

CHAPTER 7

The house was a small modern bungalow in the Barnton district of Edinburgh. The nearest neighbours were probably someone's senior management . . . Barnton was two-car garages and private schools, not quite as select or wealthy as some of the old but fashionable parts of Edinburgh. Just a lot more comfortable.

It was four-thirty when Thane stopped the Ford outside the bungalow. He got out and waited for Sandra Craig to join him from the passenger side. Although it was sunny, the wind was rustling through the little garden and sweeping stray leaves into the big open carport to one side of the house.

Shona Barry was at home. Her dark-green Fiat was in the carport, occupying less than half the space. But they also knew from a radio conversation they'd had with the Squad surveillance team, who were in a grey utility truck waiting further along the road. It had Water Department signs on its sides, the driver wore overalls, and they'd lifted a manhole cover for added effect. Around Barnton, not many people spoke to workmen anyway.

"Sir." Sandra Craig didn't look too happy. She touched his sleeve as he took a first step forward. "How hard do we push her? I mean—"

"And I've told you." Thane cut her short. They'd already talked about it on the drive through. "All we're sure about is they're brother and sister."

"But you'll go easy?"

"No, I'll work her over with a rubber hose," said Thane dourly. "That's my style, isn't it?"

They went to the front door. Instead of steps, a gently sloping concrete ramp led up to it. Glass panels gave a glimpse of a carpeted hallway with flowers on a side table. Thane rang the doorbell and Shona Barry appeared after a moment, propelling her chair towards them. She gave a surprised smile at him through the glass, then opened the door.

"Come in, Superintendent." She sounded pleased, and spun the chair clear with a flick of her wrists. "Changed your mind about helping us?"

"Maybe more the other way around." He kept his manner friendly, gestured Sandra in ahead of him, then waited until Shona Barry had closed the door again. "On your own?"

"Yes." The girl was wearing jeans and a light-brown shirt-blouse, her feet in sandals, her dark hair tied back by a band of red ribbon. She looked up at Sandra quizzically. "Not like you."

"Sorry."

He made the introduction and watched them shake hands. People like Shona Barry didn't want sympathy, and he wasn't on that kind of mission. But he felt a moment's irrational anger—these two were the same age, had the same bright, intelligent temperament, were probably alike in many other ways. Except for that wheelchair.

"So, what's the mystery?" Shona Barry faced him again, then grinned. "You're too tall to leave standing around. I'll get a crick in my neck—this way."

She wheeled ahead of them and swung in at a doorway. The room beyond was bright and tastefully furnished. Two watercolour originals hung framed on the fireplace wall, and a glass display cabinet held a carefully spaced collection of what looked like silver snuffboxes and other small pieces.

"Sit down, both of you." The girl gestured to two comfortable leather armchairs. As they settled in them, she brought herself around beside a low worktable. Among the rags and cleaning materials on it were two blackened objects which looked like saucers but with a glint of silver beginning to break through. She grimaced at the table. "Sorry about the mess. I got these in a junk shop. Now I'm trying to find out if I made a mistake."

"And if you didn't?" asked Sandra.

"Then I've bought a pair of English nineteenth-century bon-bon dishes off the housekeeping." The dark-haired girl chuckled. "Except, of course, they could be Portuguese—some Portuguese silversmiths had a nasty habit of faking English hallmarks around that time. Call it a different kind of detective work."

Thane nodded. "Lord Mackenzie said silver was your speciality."

"It would be, if I had the money," she corrected cheerfully, easing around a little to face him. "So—what's your problem, Superintendent? If it isn't Ransom Trust business—"

"Shona." Thane knew there was no sense in postponing it. "Where were you last Sunday evening?"

She blinked. "Why?"

"Just tell me."

She shrugged. "All right. I was here, at home."

"Alone?" asked Thane.

She nodded, puzzled.

"Could you prove it?" asked Sandra Craig quietly. "Any way at all?"

"If I had to, yes." There was a hint of indignation in her voice. "I phoned various people on Ransom Trust business. Right up until—well, after midnight, I suppose. They'd remember."

Thane nodded. "So you didn't use your car that night?"

"No. I couldn't have, anyway. Peter borrowed it because his own was being serviced and—" Her voice died away, then she gave a resigned sigh. "What did he do? Pick up a speeding ticket or something?"

"Just tell me how long he had the car," persisted Thane.

"From about lunchtime until—well, whenever he got back." The girl shrugged, her patience obviously at an end. "I don't know. All right, he was late and I went to bed. But that's *his* business. I'm his sister, not his wife—and no way his keeper." Spinning the wheelchair around, she placed herself with the worktable like a barrier between them. "Now, what's going on? Why the questions?"

"It's Peter." Thane watched her carefully. "We're looking for him, Shona. It looks like your brother is working with the team involved in these antiques robberies."

She didn't speak for a moment, just stared at him, her hands dropping involuntarily to the wheelchair rims and gripping them till her knuckles showed white.

"You—" She moistened her lips. "You're serious?"

"Yes." Thane reached into his pocket and brought out the set of photographs Criminal Intelligence had supplied before he left Glasgow. Getting up, he spread them on the table in front of her. "These five men, Shona—recognise any of them?"

For a moment she looked almost blindly at the faces of Goldie Boyd and his team. Then, slowly, she shook her head.

"They're the ones?" she asked in a voice that was barely a whisper, her face pale.

Thane nodded.

"But you can't be sure. About Peter, I mean—" She turned quickly to Sandra. "It could be a mistake, couldn't it?" She saw sympathy in the other girl's expression, a sympathy that gave her enough of an answer. She moistened her lips. "I don't believe it."

"You think he's in London," said Thane. "We don't. When he goes on these trips, do you know where to contact him? Does he keep in touch?"

"No. There's no need," she said tightly. "He has to travel around a lot. He knows I can look after myself."

"I'd like to see his room," said Thane. "Do I need a search warrant?"

"Don't bother." Her head came up defiantly. "Help yourself. It's across the hall, the second door."

"Thank you." He signalled Sandra to stay with the girl and went out.

Peter Barry's bedroom was modest in size, tidy, and almost the sole item on the dressing table was a framed photograph of the man and his sister. Drawing a deep breath, Thane got to work.

He searched carefully, as quietly as he could, and didn't waste time. There were a few family papers in a dressing-table drawer, but the rest amounted to neatly folded shirts and underwear, carefully hung suits, total normality. Pausing, he heard a low murmur of conversation from the other room. For the moment, he didn't envy Sandra her role.

There was a travel bag lying on top of the wardrobe. He had to bring the dressing-table stool over and stand on it to reach the bag, and when he brought it down it was locked.

It was a good lock, but on leather. Taking out his penknife, he cut around the metal, opened the bag, then froze and swore aloud.

A woman's wig, long and dark, lay on top. Beneath it was a folded dress, shoes and other clothing. Carrying the bag, he went back to the dressing table and looked again at the photograph of Peter Barry and his sister. They shared the same fine features. Wearing the wig, dressed in women's clothes, with a touch of makeup added—he nodded to himself in the dressing-table mirror.

There was no mystery left about the woman who had collected Anna Marshton in Glasgow. Or the woman who had charmed her way past those traffic cops on the road to the south.

He took the travel bag back to the other room. Shona Barry was still pale but more composed. She was smoking a cigarette, but she laid it down as he entered.

"This was on top of the wardrobe." He showed her the bag. "Recognise it?"

She nodded. "Peter keeps it there."

"Any idea what's inside it?"

"Sports gear, I think." Her voice held a bitter edge, and she gestured at her useless legs. "I'm not too good at prowling, even if I felt like it."

Silently, Thane laid the bag on her lap. As he stood back, he gave Sandra a warning glance.

"Thank you," said Shona Barry stonily. She opened the bag impatiently, then they heard her gasp.

She stared at the contents for a long time. When she looked

up, it was with an expression of total bewilderment, bewilderment which held a trace of fear.

"I don't understand." She paused, swallowed, put the bag beside her chair, then gave a shaky, forced laugh. "Look, there's nothing bent about Peter. I—I know plenty of women who can tell you that much."

"There was a murder in Glasgow," said Thane. "Witnesses thought they saw a woman. And there were other times."

Shona Barry seemed to shrink in her wheelchair. Then, suddenly, she began to shake. Getting beside her, Sandra Craig put a quick arm around her shoulders and tried to comfort the girl. At the same time, she managed to give Thane an outraged glare.

There was a drinks cabinet in the room. Thane poured some whisky into a glass and made the girl swallow it. Then he waited patiently. At last, she looked up at him again.

"Couldn't you be wrong?" she pleaded. "Are you really sure?"

"As sure as we can be, till we find him," said Thane. He paused, then asked quietly, "He didn't give you any hint that— well, anything was wrong?"

She shook her head.

"Can you think of anywhere he might be?"

"No." She moistened her lips, then added impulsively, "Even if there was, I—"

"You might not tell us?" Thane gave her a slight smile of understanding. "Think about it, Shona." He looked around. "I can't leave you on your own. Sandra will stay with you until we make a better arrangement."

The girl nodded dully. There were no tears in her eyes. Thane felt they'd come later. A girl like Shona Barry would keep real emotion as a private thing.

He touched her shoulder, then went out to the hall and the telephone.

It was after seven in the evening when Colin Thane got back to Glasgow and left his car in the Crime Squad parking lot. The building was quiet, Maggie Fyffe had gone home, Jack Hart's door was closed and locked.

His own office door was open. Francey Dunbar was inside, leaning against the windowsill, his thin, tanned face twisting a wry grin as Thane entered.

"Welcome back," said his sergeant. "I heard about Shona Barry. How did she take it?"

"Badly," said Thane shortly. "What's new here?"

"Nothing," admitted Dunbar. "Commander Hart said to pack it in for tonight."

"Right." Thane didn't object. He felt he had already had more than enough for one day. Dropping into his chair, he sat back and scowled at Dunbar. "Where the hell did you get to this afternoon?"

"Something turned up." Dunbar made a vague, apologetic noise. "I got back as soon as I could. Did—uh—did it matter?"

"No," said Thane wearily. "But next time ask first—don't just vanish." He glanced at his watch. "All right, on your way."

"Sir." Dunbar grinned, shoved himself away from the windowsill, and started for the door. As he reached it, he stopped and glanced around. "You've to call Inspector Moss at Strathclyde Headquarters. He said it's personal—he'd wait till you got back."

Thane nodded, his tiredness suddenly forgotten. Once Dunbar had gone out he carefully lit a cigarette, then lifted the telephone.

When the call got through, Phil Moss answered his extension right away. He sounded reasonably cheerful.

"I thought you'd like to know we're getting somewhere," he told Thane. "All right to talk at your end?"

"Yes." Thane's grip tightened a little on the receiver. "What's happening, Phil?"

"Your boy has a friend named Andy Lyall." Moss paused. "He could do without him. Young Lyall has other friends. A couple of them were apprentice motor mechanics until they were fired. Now it looks like they're trying their hand at the hot-car game."

Thane almost groaned. "There has been plenty of that around our place. You're sure of it, Phil?"

He waited, remembering that someone else had asked him exactly that question not so long before.

"That's how it looks," said Moss cautiously. "I've an idea about how Tommy stands in it, and you could be lucky."

"Lucky?" asked Thane flatly.

"That you found out soon enough. I've had to recruit some help on this—there's too much ground to cover. But we've got Tommy tied to Lyall, Lyall tied to the two that matter."

"What's your next move?" asked Thane.

"I've a free hand, remember?" Moss gave a chuckle. "I'm using it." The humour vanished from his voice. "Tommy probably isn't the only youngster on the fringe of this, Colin. But it could be these yobs particularly want him. Understand?"

"Maybe." Thane chewed his lip. "Because he's a cop's son?"

"Right," said Moss. "If he looks for his box in your garage, it's gone. I collected it while Mary was out. If he thinks someone stole it, fair enough—that's better than leaving him knowing someone has been inside it. Play the situation the way I asked, and I'll get back to you tomorrow sometime."

Thane thanked him and hung up.

He stayed where he was, stubbed out his cigarette, then sat for a moment with his eyes closed. Finally, he opened them again, got to his feet, and headed out of the building.

It was time to go home.

Mary met him as usual at the front door. He kissed her, heard a record player pumping out one of the current top twenty, and knew Kate was around.

"Where's Tommy?" he asked.

"Hanging about." Mary gave a puzzled shrug. "He was in his room. I think he's out in the garage again."

She'd already given the children their evening meal, but she'd waited.

"Get washed and we'll eat," she told him. "The menu is baked

trout—though, if you'd been any later, they'd have been cre-
mated in that oven."

"Would I have known the difference?" he asked innocently,
then dodged the mock swing she aimed at him. "Give me a couple of minutes."

He went looking for Tommy. He found his son in the back
garden, aimlessly kicking a ball against the garage wall.

"Hello," said Thane. "How was school?"

"Uh—the usual." Tommy gave him a wary smile.

"None of your pals available tonight?" asked Thane.

Tommy shook his head. He seemed to be waiting for Thane to
say more.

"You'll survive." Thane took an experimental kick at the ball,
managed to trap it on the rebound, then his next effort failed
miserably. "I used to be better than that—I think."

He ambled back into the house, leaving Tommy still watching
him.

The trout had emerged only slightly dried at the edges. He
kept the conversation light and general with Mary while they
ate, helped her clear up afterwards, then stayed in the kitchen
until she'd finished. Through the window, he could see Tommy
still kicking at the football.

"Mary." He waited until she turned. Then he nodded towards
the garden. "You were right. We've got a problem. Not bad trouble, if we're lucky. But I'm not sure yet."

Her face paled. "You'd better tell me."

Thane did, quietly and deliberately, leaving out nothing.
When he finished, he noticed for the first time that she was still
holding a dish towel in her hands. It had become a tight,
crushed ball. She turned away for a moment, then straightened.

"I'm glad it's Phil." She looked out of the window and drew a
deep breath. "And we—we just do nothing, say nothing?"

Thane nodded. The telephone had begun ringing, but he knew
Kate would answer it.

"Till we hear." He took the dish towel from her hands and
laid it down. "Phil knows what he's doing."

She nodded. Kate shouted from upstairs. The telephone call was for Thane. Cursing under his breath, he went to take it.

"Thane?" The thin, precise voice on the line sounded like a polite whipcrack. "Mackenzie—your Edinburgh people obliged me with your home number. You may have an idea why I'm calling."

"Yes." Thane was still surprised. He'd known Bloody Mac would get involved sooner or later, but the High Court judge hadn't wasted time. "You've heard about Barry?"

"I telephoned Shona, on Ransom Trust business. She—well, she told me enough." Lord Mackenzie was choosing his words with care. "You feel the situation is beyond reasonable doubt?"

"Well beyond," said Thane dryly.

"I see." There was a moment's silence on the line, then Mackenzie spoke again. "And could Shona's position be construed as—ah—protective custody?"

"Only by a lawyer," said Thane. "But I'm not leaving her alone."

"You've no reason to believe she's involved?"

"None," said Thane. "We're keeping an eye on her, that's all. Have you a better idea?"

"Yes." Mackenzie grabbed the opening. "I could bring her through to Drum Lodge. My housekeeper is there. She could stay until—ah—the matter is over."

Thane thought for a moment. It was a reasonable suggestion, one he liked.

"All right," he said. "Go ahead. As long as she agrees."

"Good," said Mackenzie briskly. "Tell your people I'll understand if there's the occasional police car lurking near the Lodge."

He said goodbye and hung up.

The rest of the evening passed quietly. Tommy drifted in to watch television, saying little and looking unusually worried. At last, he went early to bed.

"What's wrong with him?" asked Kate, frowning after her brother. "Is he ill or something?"

"No." Mary exchanged a glance with Thane. "Has he said anything to you, Kate?"

"He wouldn't. He's a boy," said Kate, and left it at that.

Inevitably, they talked about it again once Kate had gone to bed. Then there was nothing left, nothing but to wait.

Thane slept badly that night. He was glad when morning came with its usual rushed routine, and he left at the same time as Tommy and Kate.

He reached his office shortly before nine. Outside, the weather was dry but cloudy and cool, as if still trying to make up its mind what to do later.

The overnight reports were mostly routine. The continuing watch for Peter Barry, Goldie Boyd and the rest had drawn a continuing blank, the murder investigations in Glasgow and Edinburgh were plodding along without any real progress.

Francey Dunbar and Joe Felix arrived as usual. Sandra Craig joined them a little later. Thane talked with them briefly, then was summoned through to Commander Hart's room.

"Read this," said Hart, shoving a telex message across his desk. "It was a notion I had—it takes care of one little mystery."

The message was from Criminal Records. They'd taken the one minor conviction listed against Peter Barry and discovered that he'd refused to pay the fine imposed for his part in the antinuclear demonstration. They'd taken the thirty-day sentence and checked it against the files on Goldie Boyd and his team.

Mule Pearson had been serving time during the same period. In the same prison block.

"That gave him a contact," said Hart. "There had to be one to Goldie Boyd, somewhere."

They talked through the rest of it again. Then, at last, Hart said the thing which had been in Thane's mind throughout.

"All we can really do is sit on our backsides and wait for it to happen." He scowled and built a thin, bony steeple with his fingertips, as if adding a silent prayer. "But when it does happen, you're going to have to be ready to go in, hard and fast.

That's whether it's today, tonight, tomorrow, or—" He shrugged.

Thane nodded. It meant being on permanent standby, staying clear of anything else. The kind of waiting that came hard.

"And I want you and your team armed," said Hart. "Boyd's little army wouldn't think twice of shooting their way out of an awkwardness. Make that clear to everyone."

He did, when he went back through to the duty room. They showed no particular surprise, but Joe Felix grimaced. His technical skill in the electronics world was only matched by his hamhanded inability to even clip the edge of a target.

"There was a phone call for you," said Francey Dunbar when Thane had finished. He masked a grin. "Bloody Mac wants to see you again, at the High Court. He said coffee-break time."

Thane winced. It was something he could have done without. But it wasn't wise to tell a High Court judge to get lost, even one who was drifting into an unusual degree of involvement.

"Anything else?" he demanded.

"Well"—Dunbar gave an apologetic gesture—"I'll need to take some time off again, same as yesterday. I'll be on call if you need me. No problem."

"I can always ask Goldie Boyd to wait," said Thane sarcastically. "It has to be today?"

His sergeant nodded.

"All right," said Thane reluctantly. "But it's your head in the basket if anything goes wrong."

"Thanks," said Dunbar. "I'll remember."

A brief but savage rainstorm was hitting the city an hour later, as Thane drove in. But it had died away by the time he parked near the High Court, and there was a hopeful trace of blue sky overhead as he went into the building.

Once again Lord Mackenzie was on the bench in the north courtroom. Thane slipped in there, found a vacant seat near the back, and listened to the drone of evidence. There were two men in the dock, charged with kicking a total stranger to death after a Saturday-night quarrel. The dead man's skull was a Crown production and the witness was a pathologist, busy trading semantics with Defence Counsel.

It was a game. The kind of game that the professionals enjoyed playing, even with that skull in front of them. Thane had heard the same thing before, too many times for it to matter anymore. He glanced up at the bench and met Bloody Mac's gaze. The little judge looked almost bored as he gave the faintest of nods.

The pathologist finished his evidence, slightly ahead on points over his Queen's Counsel opponent. The next witness was a barmaid, but as she was sworn in Bloody Mac leaned over and murmured to his clerk.

Court was adjourned. As the barmaid was shepherded away, an usher located Thane. Once again he was escorted through to the private chambers at the rear of the court.

"Sit down, Superintendent," said Lord Mackenzie when they were alone. "That damned pathologist—some of these people go on forever."

The little judge looked ill-tempered. He had removed his wig, but hadn't bothered about his robes, and they flowed around him as he leaned back in his chair.

"How's Shona?" asked Thane.

"More settled." Lord Mackenzie's features became more benevolent. "I took her to Drum Lodge last night, of course. But it's been an obvious shock to her"—his dentures clicked—"to all of us. Including me. There's no word of her brother?"

Thane shook his head.

"There will be. That's inevitable." Mackenzie shook his head. "Have you considered a motive?"

"Sir?" Thane raised an eyebrow.

"Not for the people he's running with," said Mackenzie almost impatiently. "For Barry."

Thane shrugged. "Money—that's the obvious."

"With two murders along the way. I've heard." Mackenzie scowled as he spoke. "I talked to that girl last night—mostly because she wanted it. Maybe I can give you a motive, Superintendent. One that could surprise you."

"I'll listen," said Thane.

"To a private citizen?" The little judge gave a sardonic grin. "It was something she said, about Barry's 'business trips.' How often he managed to squeeze in some Ransom Trust work while he was away."

"Among other things," said Thane.

"Quite." Mackenzie didn't appreciate the interruption. "However, I took a look at the Trust accounts afterwards. They've one unusual feature over the last six months or so—a surprising number of anonymous cash donations. Large donations, Superintendent—mailed to our treasurer direct, no covering note, no explanation." He paused deliberately. "I checked the dates. They mostly arrived about two weeks after each of the antiques robberies."

Thane stared at him. "You know what you're suggesting?"

Mackenzie nodded.

It wasn't too often Thane felt lost for words. But he found it hard to grapple with the prospect dropped on him out of the blue.

"Two murders and the rest?" He didn't hide his cynicism. "What happened to coffee mornings?"

"Charity needs money," said Mackenzie. "There's a thing called inflation, Superintendent. A charity can work its heart out and still slide backwards—like the Ransom Trust has been doing." He pursed his thin lips. "Peter Barry goes through life with a sister trapped in a wheelchair, trapped there because medicine wasn't far enough advanced to help her. Causes matter to him, always have."

"You're asking me to buy the notion that he's Robin Hood with a computer?" Thane shook his head, not prepared to accept or reject. "Even supposing it might be that way—"

"Then your task doesn't change," murmured Mackenzie. He got to his feet, his long robes brushing the floor, crossed to a row of law books on a shelf, and ran a fingertip along them. "You'll find him, arrest him, and he'll come to court—not to my court. I couldn't be involved. But motives matter."

Thane looked at him grimly, waiting, deciding not to answer. The judge turned, faced him, and seemed to understand.

"No, you're wrong," he said. "If Barry is guilty he deserves justice—no more, no less, no favours." The little man so many feared as Bloody Mac considered Thane steadily. "A long time ago a learned Scottish judge put one side of the coin. He said a man can be very, very bad without being mad. I believe the reverse can be equally true, and that there's an area in between." Suddenly he held out his hand and gave an unexpected smile. "That's all, Superintendent. Good luck."

Thane rose and took the offered handshake. Then he left.

He knew he'd been given a glimpse of Lord Mackenzie few others had ever seen. That, and an insight into the loneliness of the man's role.

Perhaps it tempered his own role. He wasn't sure.

Things hadn't altered much when he got back. In the Crime Squad duty room, a set of marker pins had been removed from one of the wall maps. A target operation in the northeast had been completed. But apart from two suggested sightings of Goldie Boyd, both cleared up as false alarms, nothing else had changed.

Time crawled past. After about an hour, Francey Dunbar returned from his private expedition. A little later, Sandra took a telephone call, then announced she was going for lunch. She left the restaurant number, and it was one which raised Thane's eyebrows.

At 1 P.M., Joe Felix finished a repair job on the bits and pieces which had been lying on his desk. He went out with Francey Dunbar, and they brought back sandwiches and coffee.

Thane shared with them. As he finished, Maggie Fyffe appeared clutching a collection of paperwork and dumped it in front of him.

"You've nothing else to do, have you?" she said pointedly.

It was almost a relief to take the bundle along to his own room and start work on the dull administrative detail involved. But any interruption was welcome.

The sound of a car coming into the parking lot took him over to the window. It was a white M.G., one he hadn't seen before. He watched with amusement as Ed Sarraut got out on the driver's side, came round, opened the passenger door, and Sandra emerged. She saw Thane at his window, waved a greeting, then turned to talk to the bearded American dealer.

Thane went back to his desk. After a couple of minutes he heard the M.G. pull away again, and shortly after that the redhead came into his office, still smiling.

"Good lunch?" he asked pointedly.

"Perfect." She had a sparkle in her eyes. "Have I missed anything here, sir?"

"Work or food?" He shook his head, then noticed she had a slim jade bracelet on one wrist. "Did he bring that with him?"

"Yes." The redhead fingered the bracelet. "Like it?"

"I'd like to know what it cost." Thane laid down the wad of expense sheets he'd been checking. "Seeing him again?"

She nodded. "Before he leaves. And he says he will come over for the Ransom Trust exercise."

Thane frowned. "Did he ask—"

"Not about Peter Barry." She shook her head. "And I didn't tell him."

"Keep it that way." He looked at her, trying to keep a smile from his lips. Detective Constable Craig, standing there in the sunlight, would keep most men's minds occupied enough. "Did he say anything—that matters here, I mean?"

But Ed Sarraut hadn't. Thane let her go.

He finished the paperwork, took it back to Maggie Fyffe, and managed to coax a mug of coffee from her. He was returning to his office when he heard his telephone ringing.

It was Phil Moss.

"Some news for you," said Moss. "We've picked up a certain pair of young villains, got them on a string of car-theft charges.

They're talking—they've been using some of the kids at Tommy's school."

Thane bit his lip. "How about Tommy?"

"Let's say he'll be missing some friends," answered Moss. "We collected four of them from school at lunch break—including that kid Andy Lyall."

"Phil—" Thane's patience couldn't take any more.

"Not Tommy," soothed Moss. "He was one of the kids they leaned on and made do odd jobs—like hiding those keys." A noise like a chuckle came over the line. "Each kid thought he was the only one being shoved around. Now they know different."

"Thanks, Phil." Thane knew his voice was husky, but couldn't help it. He had just one worry left. "There was that jigger key—"

"Mary's fork?" Moss stayed unperturbed. "Pal Andy was using one. Tommy admits making one but says he never tried it. I believe him." His manner became more deliberate. "Now do me a favour. Go easy on him—the understanding parents bit. All right?"

"Right," agreed Thane. "Come out and eat again, Phil—soon."

He hung up and glanced at his watch. Tommy might be home from school, but he might get Mary first. His fingers fumbled a little as he dialled his home number and heard it start ringing.

Mary answered. He hardly got a chance to begin.

"I know." She was either laughing or crying. It was hard to be sure. "He's home. He's told me—the whole story." She broke off for a moment, then came back on the line. "He wants to speak to you. And—well, he's got a black eye, a split lip, skinned knuckles, but the only thing that's worrying him is what you're going to say."

There was a fractional pause.

"Dad?" His son sounded more than wary.

"Been fighting a war?" asked Thane mildly.

"Sorting out things." Tommy hesitated. "Dad, I—"

"Well?" Thane grinned at the receiver.

"I'm sorry."

"That's good enough." Thane nursed the receiver. "Clean fight or dirty?"

"Dirty." The young voice held a touch of pride. "I managed."

"Clean and dirty, I'm going to teach you a few tricks," Thane told him. "Just in case there's a next time."

Then Mary was back on the line.

"Can you make it home?" she asked.

He hesitated, knowing he should be there. But he had a gut feeling about the evening ahead, one he couldn't ignore.

"I can cope," said Mary, his silence enough of an answer. She sounded as if she'd expected it. "Anyway, Tommy's here."

"That's right," said Thane.

He said goodbye and hung up.

Colin Thane wasn't the only Scottish Crime Squad member who felt the same blend of instinct and unease about the night ahead.

Outside of normal shift duties, no one was specifically detailed to remain. But many did. Others came and went on vague excuses. His own team infiltrated into Thane's office, Francey Dunbar departing on another of his mysterious journeys and returning with a rolled-up sleeping bag and portable TV set. Joe Felix and Sandra made an expedition of their own to the nearest Chinese take-away restaurant and brought back enough food to feed a regiment.

Commander Hart was another who didn't go home, and although Maggie Fyffe left at her usual time, she reappeared in the late evening. By ten-thirty, she was running a nonstop coffee supply for anyone interested.

A telephone rang now and again. When it did, there was an immediate, hopeful silence until whoever took the call replaced the receiver.

But as the hands of the duty-room clock crawled around towards midnight a few gave up and drifted away. At midnight, even Thane began to wonder if they were the wiser ones.

At 1 A.M. he ran out of cigarettes and borrowed a fresh pack from Maggie Fyffe.

Three minutes later, another telephone call came in. Hart took it because he was nearest.

They saw his attitude change as he listened. He asked a couple of questions, then hung up, looked at Thane and nodded.

"We're in business." The Squad commander's lined face was a tight, unemotional mask. "There's been a container-truck hijack outside Prestwick Airport. The driver and security guard were thumped on the head and left in a ditch, another man shot."

"A truck?" Thane stared at him. "But—"

"A truck," Hart said. "Get down there. It was carrying antiques valued at two million dollars, according to the airport police. The antiques were on their way to New York—don't ask me why or where they came from."

"Two million—" Francey Dunbar swallowed. "What's that in our money?"

"Enough," said Thane.

Hart nodded.

One thing seemed sure. Peter Barry and Goldie Boyd had got their big one.

CHAPTER 8

It was thirty-two miles to Prestwick International Airport, most of it fast dual carriageway. Three cars loaded with Crime Squad personnel covered the distance in twenty-three minutes, a small convoy racing through the dark, windy night.

Colin Thane was in the lead car, with Francey Dunbar driving. They passed a few newspaper vans heading out of the city on delivery runs, and an occasional airline coach came towards them, leaving a brief impression of a glow of light and the tired, anonymous faces of jet-lagged passengers. But at that hour the only other traffic was a rare private car crawling home from some late-night party, the driver with a probable blood-alcohol problem.

Thane's car radio murmured a couple of times on the way. Back at base, Commander Hart had arranged a rendezvous point at the Monkton Roundabout, close to the airport.

A county police car was waiting at the roundabout, its blue light flashing like a beacon against the background haze of the airport's lighting. Beyond that haze was a flat blackness which was the sea.

The convoy pulled in and a uniformed figure hurried over from the county car. Thane wound down his window, and the man stuck his head in.

"Chief Inspector Williamson, sir," he said, a mixture of tension and worry etched on his lean face. "It happened about a mile from here."

"You lead," nodded Thane.

Williamson returned to his car and the convoy started off again, following the flashing blue light.

At first, they stuck with the bypass road which skirted the airport perimeter. Then they turned off, taking a side road which seemed to be heading straight for the runway lights. But suddenly it doubled back—and as they rounded the bend Thane saw police cars stopped ahead beside a parking lay-by.

The convoy halted. Getting out, hearing doors open and close as the other cars emptied, Thane went over to join Williamson, then took a quick look around.

Backed by young trees, furnished with concrete litter bins, the lay-by area had been cordoned off with a thin line of yellow tape. But inside the tape, close to the trees, a white sports car lay as if abandoned, with the driver's door half open and its lights switched off.

He knew the car. If he needed any confirmation, he heard Sandra Craig give a dismayed gasp at his side.

"Ed Sarraut's?" he asked.

She nodded, tight-lipped, and he turned to Williamson, gesturing towards the white M.G.

"What happened to the driver?"

The local chief inspector grimaced. "Shot twice—once in the shoulder, once in the chest." He gave Sandra a quick, partly comprehending frown. "His driving licence says his name is Sarraut—we got him to hospital and they're going ahead with emergency surgery. He has a chance."

"And the other two?" demanded Thane.

He had to wait for an answer as a big transatlantic jet came rumbling in over their heads. It touched down, tyres screaming, then the air vibrated as the engines went into full reverse thrust to slow its rush along the runway.

"The truck driver and his mate—" Williamson started his answer as a shout, then lowered his voice as the airliner's noise died away. "They're all right—thumped on the head and left tied." He thumbed towards the police already moving around the lay-by area. "One of our patrol-car crews saw the M.G. and stopped for a routine check. The man who'd been shot was lying beside the car, the other two had been dumped behind the litter bins."

"You've got someone at the hospital, with Sarraut?"

Williamson nodded.

The night was cold. Stuffing his hands into his coat pockets, Thane stepped over the yellow marker tape into the lay-by area. He reached the white M.G. at the same time as a police photographer, but the man gave him a wry grin and stood clear.

There was enough light coming from the other vehicles around to show the interior. An opened box of chocolates lay on the passenger seat, a few chocolates missing from the top layer. The ignition key was still in the switch, the handbrake was on, the gear lever was in neutral.

"Seen this?" asked Williamson as he drew back. The county man indicated a small, gouged hole in the M.G.'s bodywork just in front of the driver's door. "The truck driver and his mate heard three shots—that's probably the one that missed." He shrugged. "We've a full alert out for the truck—it's a big articulated Volvo unit. But this bunch had at least an hour and a half's start before we even knew about it, so—" He left the rest unsaid.

"What's the story?" demanded Thane.

"Confused," said Williamson.

"Then confuse me," said Thane grimly. Beyond them, men were making a careful search of the lay-by area using hand lamps. One group were laying strips of protective plastic over what looked like tyre tracks. "Right now, that's easy enough."

"The truck's last stop was Edinburgh—"

"Last?"

Williamson nodded. "There's a list. They'd been picking up crated antiques from collecting points, working down from Aberdeen. Different dealers, but all the stuff bound for the States."

Thane almost groaned aloud, understanding at last what had happened.

"And at Edinburgh?"

"They loaded this man Sarraut's stuff, then he announced he'd tail them through to Prestwick because he wanted to see it loaded." Williamson broke off as a sergeant came over to him. They had a brief, murmured conversation, then Williamson turned back to Thane. "Anyway, he did—follow them, I mean. They were waved down by what looked like a police car near the Monkton Roundabout, just about where I collected you."

"And the men in the car wore police uniforms?" Thane said it wearily, remembering the raid on Drum Lodge. "Hello, and follow me?"

Williamson nodded. "The story was a road diversion due to a sewer collapse, that they'd been sent to escort the truck another way into the freight terminal." He scratched his chest through his shirt and scowled. "When the truck got here, it was waved down again. Then the crew were jumped by the rest of the team."

"And Sarraut?"

"He stopped behind them, they heard the shots like I said," repeated Williamson. "Probably he tried to be a hero, but I go along with the truck driver. He got a sawn-off shotgun stuck in his guts and decided he wanted to reach pensionable age."

Thane grimaced. "No one missed them at the airport?"

"No." Williamson was emphatic. "The airline knew the truck was on its way, but the cargo flight isn't due out till dawn—and, anyway, the night shift have their meal break around midnight."

They went around the rest of the area together. The Crime Squad team had already joined the local contingent, lending a hand where they could. Mostly, that amounted to an inch-by-inch search of the area using torches and hand lamps, and two luckless constables had been assigned the task of emptying the litter bins.

There were heavy tyre marks at the edge of the tarmac and other, lighter marks which might have belonged to the bogus police car. Might—but the way any parking lay-by was used meant it was a long shot. More positive, a few footprints and some apparently fresh cigarette ends had been found on the soft ground beside the trees.

"Sergeant Dunbar—" Thane waited until Francey Dunbar answered his hail and came towards him out of the night. "Tell Joe Felix to take Sandra over to the local hospital. I want them at Sarraut's bedside when he comes out of the anaesthetic. They might get something from him."

"Sandra should, anyway," said Dunbar.

"*If* he comes around." Chief Inspector Williamson made it a warning. "There's no guarantee."

"But if he does—" Thane chewed his lip, then touched Dunbar's arm. "Better warn Joe not to rely on getting a second chance."

"Warn Joe, not Sandra." Francey Dunbar nodded impassively. Dying depositions were emotional mangles for any cop, ten times worse when there was any personal involvement. "What about the rest of us, sir?"

"Leave one car here to help the Chief Inspector's team." Thane saw a glimmer of gratitude on Williamson's thin face and knew it was a good investment. "The rest can start at the airport. Stay with them, Francey. We want to know about any strangers around the freight terminal area, anything unusual that has happened."

"What about you?" asked Dunbar, not totally pleased.

"I'm going to talk to someone about this cargo flight," said Thane.

The flight, and the truckload of antiques.

Two million dollars, close enough to spitting distance to one million pounds sterling, had come ambling down through the darkness towards the airport. Ambling down without any real escort and without any advance warning reaching the police.

He wanted to know why.

"Routine, Superintendent. Just plain routine," protested the little man for at least the third time. "Cargo gets delivered here, we shove it out on a flight, right?"

George Markson was station manager for Globe-West Air at Prestwick Airport and obviously more used to giving orders than receiving them—unless they chattered out of a telex machine.

But he'd been summoned from bed to discover a police sergeant at his door and a police car waiting outside. He'd been sensible enough to accept the invitation.

Still sleepy-eyed, almost submerged in the heavy wool sweater he wore over a shirt and trousers, he sat in his office at the airport's freight terminal and nursed a mug of black coffee between his hands. Trying hard to preserve his normal dignity, he managed a weak glare at Thane and Williamson.

"So this wasn't a special flight?" asked Thane again.

"Just one of our regular DC-8 freighters on the Prestwick–New York route," said Markson wearily. "Mixed cargo, anything legal that comes along."

"Two million dollars' worth of antiques," said Chief Inspector Williamson. "That's routine?"

"We carry gold bar sometimes. Last week we had a racehorse." Markson yawned at the manifest sheet in front of him. "We expected a truck with fourteen crates, total weight around three tons. Some were scheduled on to Boston, Chicago and Los Angeles."

Thane rubbed his forehead, feeling a dull ache building up. The station manager's office was stuffy and overheated, an airliner was warming up its jets somewhere too near for comfort, and Markson's attitude wasn't helping.

But at least the story was coming together. He'd already spoken to the truck driver and his mate, two chastened individuals who had reasons for their sore heads. Their names were Collins and Ritchie, they worked for Gordon-Vreit Security Deliveries, and the crated antiques they'd been carrying had been collected over a run that had begun at Aberdeen in the north with stops at Dundee, Perth, and a final two in Edinburgh.

That had been routine for them too. Gordon-Vreit did a similar antiques run every six weeks. The collection points might vary but the trip always ended at Globe-West Air's freight depot at Prestwick Airport. The value was none of their business. If they set out to collect fourteen crates, then that was the beginning and the end of it.

It was the first time Ed Sarraut's name had been on their collection list. But they couldn't add to what they'd already told Williamson about the hijacking. Even their descriptions of the bogus policemen were hazy.

Thane sighed and leaned forward. He could only keep on trying.

"You've got to have some documentation about what's in these crates," he insisted to Markson. "Who books the freight space with you?"

"Gordon-Vreit do it direct." Markson shuffled reluctantly through the papers on his desk. "They handle the insurance cover too—"

"Which company?"

Markson shrugged. "North British General—that's automatic. They own Gordon-Vreit, lock, stock and proverbial barrel."

Thane said nothing. He knew North British General—they handled some of his own domestic insurance but they hadn't been one of the companies affected by the earlier antiques robberies. That couldn't be chance. It had to mean that Peter Barry had deliberately avoided involving them till now.

"This is what you want." Markson found what he'd been looking for, several sheets of flimsy, close-typed forms. "We get this from Gordon-Vreit, a general listing of what's being shipped." He ran a stubby finger down one sheet and flicked over to the next. "Meissen figurines, Chinese porcelain, silver plate, gold ditto. Victorian jewellery, miniatures, crystal, jewelled tazzas—" The man looked up. "What the hell's a tazza?"

Thane glanced at Williamson. They both shook their heads.

"Well, they come expensive. Two of them, at twenty thousand dollars each." Markson pawed on through the list for a moment, then gave up. "It's not Globe-West's worry, anyway. Not when the stuff didn't reach us."

"I'm glad for you," said Thane brutally.

"Thanks." The station manager nodded, unperturbed, then pushed the list across his desk. "Take it if you want—it's no darned use to us now." He got to his feet and yawned again.

"So, unless there's anything else that can't wait till later, can I get back to bed?"

They let him go.

Abandoned and empty, the Volvo truck was found soon after dawn. That was when an early-rising farmer near Kirkconnel, a village thirty miles away over the next county border into Dumfriesshire, went to bring his herd of cows in for their morning milking and found the road between his farm and their field blocked by the big articulated unit.

He telephoned the police station at Kirkconnel to complain. He gave the truck's registration number to the sleepy-voiced village constable who took the call. Unshaven, still half-dressed, the village constable got there in ten minutes flat, then ran for his car radio.

Colin Thane got there an hour later. Francey Dunbar and Joe Felix were with him in the Crime Squad car, Chief Inspector Williamson and some of his men close behind in another.

A Dumfriesshire sergeant saluted smartly as they got out of the cars and came towards him along the narrow, potholed farm road. Still unshaven, the village constable waited in the background with the rest of the reinforcements who had answered his call.

"Where's the farmer?" asked Thane.

"Milking, sir." The sergeant grinned wryly. "He kicked up hell till we gave him a hand to get his beasts out through another field." He saw Thane's question coming and shook his head. "He heard nothing, saw nothing."

Thane nodded and stood for a moment looking at the travel-stained truck. The tractor unit was black and white, the long, box-shaped trailer unit a dull grey, its rear doors already opened, the interior a mocking, empty cavern.

When the call had come in, he'd been snatching a couple of hours' sleep on a borrowed camp bed at the airport police office. The rest of his team had also got their heads down where they could.

Only one thing that mattered had happened since they'd decided there was nothing more to gain at the freight terminal. Ed Sarraut had survived surgery. Two .38-calibre bullets had been removed from his body by the medical team and he still hadn't come around from the anaesthetic—but he was reckoned to be out of danger. Sandra Craig was still at the hospital waiting, and Joe Felix had come back, relieved by another Crime Squad man.

"Do we look it over?" asked Francey Dunbar, fidgeting impatiently at his side.

Thane glanced at Williamson. "How long till your fingerprint crew get here?"

"Half an hour at most," said Williamson. "They're on their way, sir."

"We'll go easy," promised Thane.

He led the way and clambered up into the empty trailer. The metal floor was grubby, littered with wood shavings and straw packing, and he stooped as he saw something glinting among them. It was the padlock for the rear doors. The thick metal hasp had been cut.

Shrugging, he left the trailer, went around to the cab, and used a handkerchief to open the driver's door. Inside the cab, a toy dog mascot hung from the rearview mirror and a coffee flask was still jammed into the door pocket on the passenger side.

Thane climbed up, sat behind the wheel without touching it, and scowled at the instrument panel. Then his scowl changed to a frown and he looked more closely at the two large dials which shared the centre area.

"Found something?" asked Francey Dunbar, climbing up on the cab step.

"Maybe." Thane didn't trust himself to say more. "Get Joe."

Dunbar raised an eyebrow but nodded and dropped down. In a moment, Joe Felix took his place.

"Your department," said Thane simply. He pointed to the two dials. "Name them."

"Uh—" Felix blinked. "Speedometer and tachograph, boss—standard equipment on a brute this size."

"Right." Thane pursed his lips. "And a tachograph does what?"

"Gives a readout on the driver's shift hours." Felix was still puzzled. "How long he's been driving, rest periods, speed on the road and—" His voice died away as he began to understand.

"And keeps a permanent record," said Thane. "Charts it almost like a map—if someone had to use it that way."

Felix bit his lip, then nodded. "It could be done. Not easily, but—move over, will you?"

Thane slid over into the passenger seat and Felix took his place behind the wheel. The chunkily built detective constable peered at the tachometer dial for a moment, then produced a small pocketknife. He used one of the slim blades to pick a lock on the unit, flicked a lever, and the tachometer's front dial swung open like a small round door.

"This is what you want." Reaching in, Felix brought out a paper disc like a clock face, but a clock face with a single central hole surrounded by graduated rings. Each ring held its individual inked reading in a series of jagged, graph-like lines. He considered the disc carefully. "Some of it is easy enough."

"Tell me," invited Thane.

"These flat spots." Felix pointed to the inked graph on one of the middle rings. "That's when the truck was stationary for a spell. Go down to the next ring, and you can tie them to time—the whole damned thing works on a twenty-four-hour cycle, even if the vehicle is doing nothing." He peered more closely. "According to this, the truck was dumped here about one-thirty A.M. Working back, it had a stop of half an hour around midnight—"

"When it was unloaded," said Thane.

Felix nodded, and moved his finger further back around the scale. "And there's where it was grabbed in the lay-by." Having got going, he became more expansive. "What you have are three inked stylus tips registering distance, speed and driving mode, getting most of it from the gearbox."

Thane stopped him. "Can you tell where it's been? That's what matters."

"Yes, but the slow way—by deciding where it hasn't been." Felix sucked his teeth for a moment. "Where you've got a steady road speed registered, that means the driver has been cruising along, main-road style. When there's a jumble, he's had to stop at a junction or at least slow down for a tight turn. We tie it all into time and distance, try and plot it back on a decent map—" He stopped, grinned, and nodded. "Give me time, maps and a magnifying glass and I'll do it."

"Accurately?" asked Thane.

"Enough to bet on it," said Felix. "These things register just about anything down to a driver blowing his nose." He saw Thane's doubt. "I mean it. A real expert could probably tell you what the weather was like on a regular route."

"The weather we know," said Thane. "What about deciding where it hasn't been?"

"That's what takes time," said Felix patiently. "Suppose the final reading shows the truck stopped after travelling steadily for a hundred yards—and we can go finer than that. We go back the way, to a peak in the graph that has to mean a stop or a slow at a road junction. We find the road junction, fine. But the truck could have got there from either of two directions, right? And the previous steady distance was three hundred yards—"

"So you go back again." Thane gave a silent, appreciative whistle of understanding. "You measure in reverse along the choice of approaches—"

"And find the one that fits, with a junction three hundred yards back," said Felix, beaming. "That's putting it crudely, boss. You've got to remember steep hills, a bad bend, things like that. Still, it's simple—isn't it?"

"I'll believe you." Thane thumbed towards the cab door. "Move. The airport should have maps, and anything else you need."

Outside, he called Chief Inspector Williamson over and tried to explain as briefly as he could. To say Williamson looked doubtful would have been charitable, but he was more than willing to wait with the truck. By then, Francey Dunbar had the Crime Squad car turned in the narrow road with the engine running and Joe Felix aboard.

Thane joined them, and Dunbar set the car moving with a squeal of rubber and a spatter of gravel.

A few miles down the road they met the cars taking out the fingerprint and forensic squad. Dunbar swept past them without slowing, giving a brief horn-blast greeting.

Above the noise of the engine, Thane heard a strange sound coming from behind him. He glanced around. Joe Felix was sprawled back on the rear seat, singing to himself in a dreadful off-key.

It was a hopeful sign. Thane grinned, told him to shut up, and wasn't surprised to be totally ignored.

In terms of passenger traffic, Prestwick Airport features well down the international league table. But there had been thick fog in the London area that morning almost exactly as the overnight transatlantic flights began to arrive—and one reason for Prestwick's existence was that kind of situation.

A steady stream of aircraft, flag carriers for nations on both sides of the Atlantic, began coming in on diversion from Heathrow and Gatwick. Touching down one after another on the long main runway so close to the sea, they began to pack the apron and dispersal areas. Baggage crews toiled, customs and immigration squads sweated as several thousand unexpected arriving passengers were dumped on their laps.

It was 9 A.M. when Thane's car reached the terminal. By then, a horde of bewildered travellers were swamping the inquiry desks. Airline staff summoned coaches, sought hotel rooms, and coped with more work than usually came their way in a month.

Battling through it all, the three Crime Squad men reached the comparative quiet of the airport police office. The duty sergeant there listened to what they wanted, nodded, and got to work. He managed to produce an empty room and a large table for Joe Felix. He produced a collection of ordnance maps, disappeared briefly, and returned with a magnifying glass borrowed from the medical room.

Joe Felix was happy. Leaving him to it, Thane and Francey Dunbar closed the door behind them as they went out.

Leaning on a balcony rail, they were looking down at the chaos in the main concourse area when Dunbar nudged Thane and pointed. For a moment Thane caught only a glimpse of red hair, then Sandra Craig came up a busy stairway, saw them, and came over.

"I've been trying to find you," she said accusingly, and frowned at the milling passengers. "Who dreamed this lot up?"

"The weatherman," said Dunbar. "How's your patient?"

"Improving." She turned to Thane. "Ed came out of the anaesthetic about an hour ago—he's sleeping now."

"Good." Thane knew Sandra Craig had been awake most of the night, yet she hardly showed it. "Did you manage to talk with him?"

"Yes." She gave a quick smile. "For a minute or two, anyway. He wasn't too sure he was alive at first."

"Then he saw you?" suggested Dunbar.

"Go to hell, Sergeant," she said, then faced Thane again. "I had to tell him how much the stuff in that truck was worth—he didn't know. He'd just heard that other American antique dealers used the same collection run and decided to join in."

"But he still suddenly decided to go along as an escort," reminded Thane, frowning.

"He says that was curiosity." She shrugged. "I think he was beginning to worry, but he won't admit it."

"That can wait." Thane pursed his lips. "What about when they were ambushed?"

Sandra grimaced. "Ed just saw what was happening and didn't stop to think. He says he hit one of them fairly hard, then saw another coming at him with a gun, the man who shot him." She paused. "He was one of the two in police uniforms, and he came right into Ed's headlight beams."

Thane tensed. "So Sarraut got a good look at him?"

She nodded. "Thin face, high cheekbones, and a mouthful of gold fillings."

"Goldie Boyd." Thane gave a slow, satisfied nod, then laid a hand on her arm. "Better get some rest. You've earned it."

"Rest?" She looked surprised and hurt. "I haven't had breakfast yet. Don't I get to eat first?"

Thane heard Francey Dunbar chuckle. From where they stood, he could see the airport cafeteria was under siege. But there was an upstairs restaurant, where the prices kept things quieter. He thought briefly and sadly about what it would do to his expense sheet, then sighed and led the way.

By midmorning the flood of diverted incoming flights had died down and the airport was struggling back to normal. There were only a few stragglers complaining around the inquiry desks, and the airport police were left with nothing more serious than a handful of complaints about disappearing luggage and a lost child whom no one seemed to want to claim.

The pressure off, they turned over more office space to their Crime Squad lodgers. Along the corridor, Joe Felix was still immersed in his maps, but stopped tapping on a pocket calculator long enough to ask Thane to get him a local police patrol car driver. Then, making it plain he wasn't welcoming visitors, he got back to work.

It took about ten minutes for the patrol car driver to arrive. As the man vanished into Joe Felix's temporary lair, Thane had a telephone call from Commander Hart in Glasgow.

"Just keeping you informed," said Hart. "North British Assurance say Peter Barry did help with their computer installation, just like the others. They've also been giving insurance cover to this damned Gordon-Vreit collection run for the past couple of years."

"But never thought to tell us, either of them?" said Thane in disgust.

"No." Hart gave a short, humourless bark of a laugh. "I quote.

'We usually prefer to keep a low profile.' Except they don't feel that way now. What's happening with you?"

"No change," said Thane.

He finished the call and hung up. No change meant that every police force in the country now had descriptions of Peter Barry, Goldie Boyd and the rest of their team—and the warning they were armed and dangerous.

It meant vehicles being stopped and searched at traffic arteries like the European sea route through Stranraer to Ireland. It meant checkpoints on roads, swoops on lorry parks—a whole wide area virtually sealed off.

For six men and three tons of antiques, vanished without trace.

He lit a cigarette. Across the room, Francey Dunbar was lounging in a chair. Dunbar was in his shirtsleeves, the holstered Smith and Wesson .38 at his hip jutting out at an uncomfortable angle.

"Coffee?" suggested Dunbar.

Thane nodded. Dunbar got up. As he reached the door, it opened and Chief Inspector Williamson came in. The county man's shoes were covered in mud and he grimaced at Thane's unspoken question.

"Forensic are finished at the truck," he reported. "They've got nothing worth a damn." He flopped down in the chair Dunbar had vacated. "How's it coming with that tachograph notion?"

Thane shook his head.

It was another half hour before they found out. Then the door burst open again and this time Joe Felix stuck his head around.

"Like to come through?" he asked.

He didn't have to repeat the invitation. They followed him through to the other room. Somehow appearing out of nowhere, Sandra Craig was with them as they crowded in.

Three large-scale maps were spread on the table. The others had been discarded. His uniform tunic unbuttoned, a satisfied grin on his face, the patrol car driver stood discreetly in the background.

"I had a problem." Felix blinked at his audience almost apologetically. "Still, that's inevitable, I suppose." He beamed at Thane. "I can explain the principle again, and—"

"No." Thane swallowed his impatience. "Just show us what you've got."

Felix sighed, picked up a pencil, and used it like a pointer on the nearest of the maps.

"We start here, where the truck was abandoned. Then, translating the tachograph readings and working backwards, this is how they got there—" As he spoke, the pencil traced its way through a maze of minor roads and crossings. Before he finished speaking, he was on the second map. Looking up, he commented, "That was the easy part."

Thane hardly heard. He was watching the moving pencil. The route it was tracing amounted to a looping curve, a curve gradually heading westward, coming closer to the area around the airport.

"Now." Suddenly Felix tapped a spot on the second map. "This is where it got really tricky. The tachograph disc showed what could have been a halt at a junction, except there was nothing like that on the map. If I was wrong there, the whole thing was out of kilter." He grinned across at the patrol driver. "Our friend helped—he knows the spot. It's not a junction, but roadworks, with temporary traffic lights and a single lane working. So—" Swiftly, he crossed to the last map. "A few minor problems after that, as we go like this, and this—" The pencil raced again. Then he paused deliberately, grinned, and brought the pencil down sharply. "And we're here. The only real stop after the hijack, and it was for half an hour. That's where they unloaded."

Thane pushed around beside him and peered at the spot Felix's pencil was touching. It was to the south, beyond Prestwick and the neighbouring town of Ayr, on the edge of the coastline. The map showed a short length of minor road leading down to the sea.

"That's at Culzean Bay," said Williamson, pushing in beside

him. Another glance was enough for the county man. "Hell, you've got them at the old Cairnrig place."

"You know it?" asked Thane sharply.

"Yes." Williamson exchanged a slight grin with the patrol car driver. "We had to clear a batch of freak-out kids from it last summer. It doesn't amount to much—a couple of ruined cottages and an old storage shed. A farmer used to use it as a barn, but it's been abandoned for years. That's where the kids moved in." He whistled softly through his teeth, for a moment, thinking. "It would fit. Nobody lives within a mile of that place."

"How far from here?"

"Fifteen, sixteen miles." Williamson raised an expectant eyebrow. "Well?"

Thane nodded. "We'll try it."

Half an hour later, the sun warm on his back, Colin Thane lay on his stomach behind the shelter of a clump of gorse bush and slightly adjusted the focus of the binoculars he was using. Immediately in front of him the ground fell away on the start of a long, gradual slope which continued until it met the sea. In distance, it was about a quarter of a mile. At the bottom, not much more than a stone's throw from the beach, was "the Cairnrig place."

Williamson had described it well. The tumbledown remains of the two old cottages were overgrown with weeds. Near them sat the storage shed. It was a rusting corrugated-iron structure, big and dilapidated, looking barely wind- and waterproof. The large double doors and a small side door lay closed. The few windows along its length were blanked out by what looked like sacking.

He heard a soft curse beside him. Francey Dunbar swore again, wriggled, and slapped an offending insect which had landed on his arm.

"Those bite," complained Dunbar. He scowled down at the shed. "What do you think?"

Thane shrugged. He brought the binoculars around in a slow sweep, ignoring the scenery and the way the sea sparkled under the clear blue sky. The road he'd first seen on the map, the road which had brought them down towards Cairnrig, continued down the slope in a slight curve which took it to the storage shed, and then on from there to an old stone landing stage at the water's edge.

"They could have been and gone," muttered Dunbar. "I— hell!"

Thane had already caught the movement at the edge of his field of vision. He swung the binoculars back as the small door at the side of the shed opened. A man came out and took a quick glance around. Then, moving a few paces, he spent a minute or so relieving his bladder against the side of the shed before going back in. It was Mule Pearson. Thane had a clear view of his face before the door closed again.

"Oh ye of little faith," murmured Dunbar regretfully. He grinned at Thane. "Sorry."

They crawled back from the edge of the slope, then jog-trotted the rest of the distance across the rough ground to where two of the Crime Squad cars and a county car were waiting. The third Crime Squad car and its crew had remained back at the airport in reserve.

Thane counted heads. Add Williamson and the three local constables he'd brought along, and his little force was twelve strong. His eyes strayed to Sandra Craig for a moment. The redhead wouldn't allow herself to be left out of anything, he knew. But seeing her standing there started a thought in his mind. It kept growing while he briefed the group on what he'd seen.

There was a problem. One which Williamson put into words before he could.

"It's not easy. Whatever way you try going down that slope, there's no cover." The man frowned. "We know they're armed. If they're keeping any kind of a lookout—" He left it there.

Thane nodded. "I wasn't planning any kind of cavalry charge. But we could give them something else to worry about." He looked pointedly at Dunbar and Sandra. "Something like you two."

"With us doing what?" asked Dunbar suspiciously.

"Brightening their lives. Like strolling hand-in-hand along that beach towards them, as a starter." Thane raised a quizzical eyebrow in Sandra's direction. "Well?"

"Why not?" She turned demurely to Dunbar. "I'm ready. But don't get too enthusiastic or I'll bat your ears off."

There were terns feeding along the shoreline, small piping birds who were more annoyed than frightened when two figures came walking along the beach. They rose briefly, calling angrily as the couple passed, then settled again.

Watching from the slope above, hidden by the gorse, Joe Felix chuckled as Francey and Sandra came on. Through the binoculars he saw Dunbar's arm around the girl's waist and her head resting on his shoulder. He decided it looked very convincing.

Suddenly Sandra broke free. Chasing her, shouting and laughing, Francey caught up close to the landing stage.

By then Felix had the binoculars trained on the shed. A sacking curtain moved at a window and a face peered out. On the beach, Francey and Sandra were now lying on the sand in an apparently passionate embrace.

Turning, Joe Felix raised an arm in a signal.

Colin Thane was alone in the lead car. He started it moving along the narrow road with the engine barely ticking over. Behind him, the other two police cars began to follow at the same gentle pace.

He moistened his lips at the start of the long downward slope, then tightened his grip on the steering wheel as his car gradually gathered speed. His eyes briefly registered the two figures still there on the beach, then his whole interest became the murmuring car and the long bulk of the shed below.

The speedometer needle was still rising as he reached the last curve, and the rearview mirror showed the other cars in close station behind.

The last curve. One hundred yards from the shed, Thane

flicked down into second gear, slammed his foot hard on the accelerator, and the car rocketed forward. As gravel spat from the wheels and the engine roared, he aimed for the centre of those big double doors.

The impact came seconds later, a splintering crash which sent them hurtling back, partly torn from their hinges, while the car lurched through into the shadows beyond. Thane braked hard, caught a glimpse of two figures trying to jump clear, then saw one hit and thrown as the car skidded to a halt.

By then he had the driver's door open and threw himself out, rolling as he hit the earth floor.

Shouts and curses echoed in the shed, then were drowned by the twin blasts of a shotgun. The car's glass disintegrated, pellets scythed the air above his head, and from outside came the squeal of brakes as the other cars arrived, a rush of feet as their crews came dashing in.

Hauling out the Smith and Wesson .38 from his waistband, Thane half-rose seeking a target. But it was over already, over as quickly as it had begun.

Moaning softly, the man hit by the car moved feebly where he'd been thrown. Another stood as if turned to stone, still holding the emptied sawn-off shotgun in one hand, two fresh cartridges clutched in the other. Two others had backed against the wall, their arms raised in surrender.

Thane reached the man with the shotgun, ripped it from his grasp, and tossed the weapon away. It was Shug Gordon, the burly, heavy-muscle member of Goldie Boyd's team. The man on the ground was Mule Pearson, the other two already being handcuffed were the breaking-and-entering duo, Tam Amos and Willie Laird.

"Where's Goldie?" demanded Thane.

Shug Gordon spat deliberately at Thane's feet.

Thane half-turned, looking around again. There were two cars in the shadows at the far end of the shed, but some of his men were already there.

He heard a warning cry, recognised Sandra's voice, and

glanced back. Shug Gordon's right hand had flickered to the back of the man's neck and he was drawing out a long, thin sliver of steel from a concealed sheath under his jacket collar.

The sharpened bicycle spoke, adhesive taped to form a grip at one end, started to swing in a raking needle-tipped arc. Simultaneously, a pistol snapped viciously from somewhere very near. The bullet smashed the thug's elbow to a bloody pulp of flesh and bone and Gordon gave a high-pitched scream, then staggered back.

Two uniformed men grabbed him. Carefully, Thane picked up the dropped bicycle spoke and looked across at Sandra Craig. Her knuckles were still white as she held her .38 in a tight, unlowered, two-handed grip.

"Thanks," said Thane.

She drew a deep breath, nodded, then lowered the pistol. Before he turned away, Thane saw her hands had begun to shake.

Williamson had been examining Mule Pearson's injuries. He got up, unimpressed, and signalled one of his men to take over.

"A broken leg, not much more," he reported to Thane. "Still, that's two hospital cases. We'll need an ambulance." Pausing, he frowned as Thane gave him the sharpened spoke. "Nasty."

"It killed a man in Edinburgh." Thane spoke tightly, trying to hide some of his disappointment. "Let's see what we've got."

He waited until their four prisoners had been pushed or dragged into a tight group, then eyed them grimly. He saw Williamson raise an eyebrow and nodded. He had to leave no loopholes. Taking a step forward, he recited the formal, inevitable caution.

"I am going to make charges against you. I have to caution you. Be perfectly clear in your mind. You are not required to make any reply in answer to these charges unless you wish to do so. But any reply you do make will be taken down in writing and may be given in evidence. Understood?"

Mule Pearson was still groaning. But the others, even Shug Gordon clutching his shattered arm, showed no reaction.

"The charges are murder, conspiracy to murder, assault, and robbery—for now," said Thane. "Anything to say?"

They stood silent. He'd expected it. Later would be different. Given time, at least one of them would talk. But time was a luxury he could afford.

"Take over," he told Williamson and walked quickly to the far end of the shed and the two cars.

Francey Dunbar was there and Joe Felix had just arrived. They were examining the cars, one a dark-blue Ford and the other a red Austin station wagon. The Ford had been the fake police car—a collection of plastic strips still lying on the back seat, some with POLICE painted on them, showed how it had been done. A dismantled blue roof light lay beside them.

"Like to look at this?" asked Francey Dunbar in an oddly puzzled voice.

Thane joined him at the station wagon's opened tailgate. Dunbar was rummaging in a large cardboard box. He'd already taken out a portable typewriter, a label-stapling gun, and a tin of black paint. Glancing at Thane, saying nothing, he laid a small paintbrush beside them. The hairs of the brush were still wet and sticky with paint.

"Look around," said Thane quietly. "You know what we want."

It was Joe Felix who found a soft patch in the earth floor nearby. When he scraped down a couple of inches, he brought out a plastic bag filled with a crumpled collection of Gordon-Vreit shipment labels from the missing antiques crates. At the bottom of the bag, still sticky with black paint, torn to pieces, they retrieved a stencil cutout. Fitted together, it read: MACHIN-ERY PARTS. FROM INTERCAST MFG. SCOTLAND.

"The full relabelling bit," murmured Francey Dunbar. "And now they're on a truck somewhere." He scowled across the shed towards the waiting prisoners. "No luck with them?"

"Did you expect it?" Thane answered absently, fumbled for his cigarettes, and lit one. He was thinking of the typewriter, thinking suddenly, for a reason it took him a moment or two to grasp, of a worried boy and a bunch of ignition keys. "Francey, suppose you were planning to get rid of these crates, fast. How would you do it?"

"Damned if I know," confessed Dunbar.

"Suppose there was a way," said Thane softly. "As offbeat as—well, a sneak-thief hiding his loot in the local cop's garage."

"Go on." Dunbar stared at him.

"Send it out air freight, from where it was stolen. Booked in advance, paperwork almost completed—and you bring a typewriter along to fill in the last few details. Every cop we've got is looking for stuff moving out of the area—not crates arriving there."

He threw down his cigarette, mashed it under heel, and went back to the prisoners and their watchful escort.

"Intercast Manufacturing—" He spoke curtly, watching them. "Does Barry think they'll really believe that at the airport?"

His shattered arm roughly bandaged, Shug Gordon glared stubbornly ahead. Mule Pearson didn't bother to look up from where he was lying. But the other two exchanged a quick, startled glance and he knew he was right.

"How long since they left?" demanded Thane. He saw Tam Amos moisten his lips and concentrated on him. "How long?"

"About an hour," answered Amos in a weary, resigned voice. He shrugged at his companions. "Hell, what's the difference now?" No one answered and he faced Thane again. "The crates are booked on a freight flight to Amsterdam."

"I'll cope here," said Chief Inspector Williamson, who'd been listening. He gave Thane a small, understanding smile. "They're yours."

Thane beckoned Francey Dunbar. Joe Felix and Sandra at their heels, they headed for the nearest serviceable car.

The few miles to Prestwick Airport were barely time enough for the string of radioed messages which had to pass between the car and the Crime Squad reserve team still at the airport police office.

But as the terminal buildings came in sight ahead, Colin Thane already knew that the freight area had been quietly and totally sealed off from the rest of the airport and the outside world—and that his last doubts had been removed.

A rented truck was unloading crates of machinery bound for Amsterdam. The two men who had driven it in and who were now sorting out the paperwork details matched the descriptions of Peter Barry and Goldie Boyd.

They coasted to a gentle halt at the freight area entrance, where a Crime Squad man was waiting. The main gate was closed. A couple of airport police stood nearby, to make sure it stayed that way.

The Crime Squad man's name was Powell. Relieved, he met Thane as they left the car. He was carrying a small two-way radio in one hand.

"We managed to tip off the freight office, sir." As he spoke, Powell guided them through a small side gate. "They've been stalling them on the documentation. But most of the crates are unloaded."

He led the way at a jog-trot, Thane and the others following. They crossed in front of one building, down the side of another, then Powell stopped as a long warehouse building appeared ahead.

"That one?" asked Thane.

Powell nodded. "On the far side. We slipped two men into the next loading bay. But—well, if there's trouble—"

Thane knew what he meant. There would be airport workers around, unaware of the danger.

"You two." He pointed to Joe Felix and Sandra. "Take the left side. Francey stays with me, we move first."

They nodded and started running.

"Pass the word we're going in," he told Powell.

As the man began speaking into his radio, Thane and Dunbar sprinted down the right-hand side of the warehouse. They reached the end, stopped and looked around the edge of the building.

Thirty yards away, a big blue rental truck was backed up to a platform. Several wooden crates had already been stacked on the platform, and a small squad of airport workers were unloading the next, using a forklift truck.

Thane ignored them for the moment. Two men were standing beside the truck cab. Both wore overalls. But one was Peter Barry. The other man had a thin, hard face, high cheekbones and receding hairline.

Peter Barry said something. Goldie Boyd nodded, but looked almost bored.

"Now," said Thane quietly.

His .38 was in his hand, held low at his side, as he stepped out. He sensed as much as saw Francey Dunbar close beside him.

They took half a dozen steps before Barry took a casual glance and saw them. He cried out in surprise, grabbing at Boyd's arm.

Then, suddenly, someone was shouting to the work squad to get clear, and they abandoned everything in a wild scramble to obey.

Boyd was first to move. He started towards the front of the truck, one hand pulling a gun from his overalls as he went. Then he froze, seeing other figures heading towards them from the far side.

He hesitated while Thane and Dunbar came on at the same steady pace. Then, with a curse, he tossed the gun away.

The sound as it hit the tarmac seemed to break the spell which had kept Peter Barry frozen where he stood. He began running, not looking back, heading blindly away.

"Francey—" Indicating Boyd, leaving him to deal with the man, Thane dashed in pursuit of the young, fair-haired figure sprinting so desperately ahead.

As he ran, he heard shouts and knew they were being followed. But there was no one else near and the gap stayed wide as, pursued and pursuer, they ran between buildings and down the side of a hangar block.

A string of aircraft were parked ahead. Maintenance men

working on the nearest stared and shouted, their voices drowned by the spluttering roar as another in the line had its engines coaxed to life.

But Barry saw them. He took one quick glance back at Thane, then veered towards the edge of the hangar block. Reaching it, he seemed to hesitate, then dashed out.

A squeal of brakes cut across the noise of the aircraft's engines. But nothing could stop the big refuelling tanker wagon in time. One moment Peter Barry was in front of it, the next he had vanished under its wheels before it could halt.

Sickened, gasping for breath, Thane ran the last few yards. He got there as the refuelling tanker's driver, white-faced and shocked, climbed down from his cab.

"He didn't give me a chance, mister." The driver was young, blue-eyed, and seemed about to be sick as he saw the crushed, lifeless thing on the tarmac under his vehicle. "He"—he swallowed hard and clutched Thane's arm—"he saw me. He looked at me an'—an' he just kept coming. Like he *wanted* it to happen."

"Maybe he did," said Thane.

He put the .38 away as others began arriving. Joe Felix was one of them, and after a few minutes he left him in charge and walked very slowly back towards the warehouse.

The news had got there ahead of him, but Goldie Boyd, handcuffed, was sitting on the platform with a disinterested air. Standing beside him, Francey Dunbar gave a grim nod as Thane arrived.

"That's it, then," said Dunbar. He turned to Boyd. "On your feet."

"No hurry." Boyd gave him a cynical, gold-toothed sneer of a grin. "Hell, I should have known better, friend. Never team up with a lousy amateur—right?"

Dunbar looked dispassionately at Boyd as he got to his feet. Then he hit him once, just once, hard in the stomach, his fist like a piston rod.

"Don't call me friend," he said wearily as Boyd doubled up. "I don't like it."

It was early evening when Thane returned home. He sat with his head against the seat, eyes almost closed, as Francey drove down the street towards the house.

There was plenty still to do. Statements, final charges, a mountain of sorting out. Back at Prestwick, a high-level wrangle was going on about whether a set of crates should still go out on the night flight to Amsterdam to see how they were collected, where they were taken, who were the buyers at that end.

He had decided he couldn't face Shona Barry. Bloody Mac was going to do that.

For the rest—he sighed to himself. Peter Barry was dead, probably because he'd wanted it that way. There would never be any way to find out where those cash donations to the Ransom Trust had come from. Goldie Boyd and his team certainly didn't know.

He sat upright as Francey nudged him and the car began to slow.

Tommy was in the front garden, pushing a grass mower up and down with an expression of dogged determination. He stopped as he saw the car and came over to the gate.

Thane got out, closed the passenger door, and Tommy grinned at him. Then he looked past him and gave a shyer smile.

"Hi, Francey."

"Hi, there," said Francey Dunbar through the opened driver's window. "How goes it?"

"No problems," said Tommy firmly.

Detective Sergeant Dunbar chuckled, winked, and set the car moving.

"When did you meet him, Tommy?" asked Thane with a sudden suspicion.

His son looked surprised. "He—well, he sorted things out. You know—at school. The trouble."

"Did he?" Thane put an arm around his son's shoulder and looked after the departing car. "Remember I told you I'd teach you some tricks—clean and dirty? I think—yes, I think we could get some help on that. From an expert."

They went into the house together.

Bill Knox is a popular and prolific mystery writer, the author of numerous novels and television scripts. He alternates stories about Detective Inspector Colin Thane with tales of Webb Carrick and the Scottish Fisheries Protection Service. A native Scot, Mr. Knox lives in Glasgow with his wife and three children.